Change

Directions

Perceive It, Believe It, Achieve It

Georges Philips

Foreword by

Dr. Edward de Bono

Change Directions
American English Edition

First published 2011

ISBN-13: 978-1904928003

ISBN-10: 1904928005

Published by Copeland and Wickson

Dedication.

To Lyndy, my wife, partner, friend and lover.

Thank you for making my life beautiful.

Acknowledgments

The inspiration for this book came from the master of thinking himself, Edward de Bono: your work has and continues to inspire and drive me. Thank you.

I would like to thank Steve Finch, for your contributions and encouraging pearls of wisdom, and Nigel Newman, for your constant uplifting words and unwavering support.

I would also like to thank Simon Shawcross, Lidia Miklis, Stephen Roachford, Stephen Broadhurst, Valerie Wiggins and Manmohan Bahra for your support and being there to test and explore the philosophy and methodology of this book.

Special Thanks

This book might never have been written had it not been for the surgeon Martin Hayward who, with his medical team at the London Heart Hospital, skillfully fixed my damaged heart and gave me another chance at life. Thank you.

Thank you to the team at Barnet General Hospital, who took care of me.

Thank you to Dr. Kim Lumley MD for his continued care for my welfare.

Foreword

Change Directions

This is, above all, a very practical book. There is an adequate amount of inspiration, but in the end the emphasis is on the practical process of changing direction.

The first part of the book analyses different situations involving change. There are those who really want to change but do not know how. There are those who have considered change but are discouraged by the risk. There are those who have not considered change because they perceive it as being too difficult. This book has something to say to all of them.

The second part of the book goes through the specific thinking and action steps that are needed in order to change direction. Each step is clear and powerful.

I would recommend this book to anyone considering change and also to all those who wonder why they are not considering change.

In the end it is your thinking fuelled by your determination that brings about a change of direction.

Edward de Bono

Prologue

Change is not a tangible object that can easily be described. It is often unpredictable and certainly inevitable. Perhaps it can be best understood as being "the" process that results in things being different.

Most people fear the idea of change yet it seems they want life to be different. Life being different *is* change. Perceiving it in this way may help minimize unnecessary anxiety.

Change Directions is not so much about adaptive changes that we are not obliged to follow, nor is it about changes that are enforced upon us; it is more about the changes that we can design, direct, implement and maintain.

The difference that can *make* the difference in the change process is you. You have and will further develop the skills and resources to design and instigate new ways that perhaps you thought were not possible.

It is prudent to make and take the time necessary to design your future, as some of the changes you are likely to make could be life changing.

It is possible that you may experience a degree of resistance to your desires for change. This is quite normal and understandable and you need not consider this in any way unusual.

On one hand we want things to change; on the other we mostly want them to stay the same. There is an expectation by some that other people or situations need to change first before we engage in the process.

Years go by, and before we know it we reach our terminus waiting for things to change in the way we would have wanted them to. In most ways, things will have changed, though not necessarily in the way we would have wanted.

Is it not strange that, with all we could possibly change, we choose to do little to invite and encourage it? The reason for this unease is explained in this book, as are the steps required to get you in the driving seat of your life.

My objective in respect to the outcome of this book is that you will at the very least experience a better understanding of the change process and, at best, transform your life into the one you have always dreamed of.

If you would like to explore the possibility that you can experience life differently then there will need to be a change in the direction you are heading. Change direction, and you will change your life.

Be assured that few have managed to accomplish greatness without developing a habit of curiosity. Just remain curious and open to the possibilities that are proposed.

Enjoy the journey.

Introduction

Change Directions was inspired by the work of Dr Edward de Bono. In his book *Teach Yourself to Think*, he describes the importance of directing attention - a must if we are to affect change in our lives by design.

Although my interest in the working of the mind originally stemmed from studying the works of Sigmund Freud, Carl Jung, Fritz Perls, Friedrich Nietzsche and Richard Bandler, it was not until I read Dr. De Bono's *The Mechanism of the Mind* that I better understood how the mind functions.

This newfound clarity inspired me to write about and teach change methods, and develop a methodology to simply reshape perception.

Additionally, by combining my knowledge of psychoanalysis, Neuro-linguistics and belief restructuring, it was possible to give life to *Change Directions*.

As a point of interest in addition to a number of other qualifications, I am also a qualified Edward de Bono systems teacher and trainer. I have authored and co-authored a number of books on the subject of change in a therapeutic setting.

The journey to discovering the drivers and motivation for change can be exciting if it is approached with an open and curious mind. At this point it may be useful to set aside any need to defend your current way of thinking.

Often when we are defending or attacking we are likely to experience a degree of fear. To maximize the benefit of this book it is advisable to place your mind in a state of curiosity and intrigue. This not only diminishes the fear but also helps the mind to explore options better suited to your current and future needs.

The style I have adopted in writing this book is one that I believe will help you to absorb the information more efficiently. The paragraphs are kept reasonably short and deliver the information in bite-size chunks to enable you to better digest.

Chapter 1

In the early Sixties, I unleashed the power of my mind. My situation had to change. Things had to be different. It took many years to fully understand the effect of my actions, but unknowingly, I engaged in the process of change.

My personal circumstances were extremely difficult at the boarding school I was sent to. I didn't speak the language, and I misunderstood the cultural rules and the political games of teachers. Lacking the experience of favoritism and the pecking order were just a few of the hurdles I needed to overcome.

The more serious challenges included bullying and other forms of inappropriate behavior. My immediate difficulty was how to deal with other boys, who were up to three years older than me. They knew the game, how to play it and how to stay safe and win.

Bullying and prejudice were normal at the boarding school. The situation reached a critical level and I felt that I was done for. No one seemed to understand the daily fear I lived with. Seeking justice and a sense of fair play was not an option. I had to find another way to survive.

I was reading a comic one day when an advertisement that promoted muscular development courses for the weak caught my attention. An image of a big, strong man appeared as part of the advertisement. The image accompanying the advertisement was that of Charles Atlas, the strongest man in the world, with the Earth held over his shoulders.

I recall cutting out the picture of him and sticking it on a window that directly faced my bed. The thought was simple: if I become as big and strong as he was, then no one would be able to bully me. It is my first recollection of setting my sights on a solution.

Nothing else had seemed to work. I had run away several times, I became obedient, cried, joked, played along, gave things away and more. Nothing had helped the situation.

Whilst lying in bed one night I imagined what it would be like to be so big and strong that no one could bully me. Later I realized that this was what my mind was focused on. One day the sticker on the window vanished, and I soon forgot all about it. I seemed to move on to other things, and I did not pay a lot of attention to the fact that when playing cricket, hockey, football, etc., I was changing. I was learning how to throw hard, how to hit hard, how to push hard.

By the beginning of the second year, I had become a formidable force to be reckoned with. I had grown more muscular and developed an attitude that resulted in other kids giving me a wider berth when walking in the corridors.

I had developed a reputation of being a little "off the wall". I became very aggressive at the first sign of being attacked and stood up to anyone who bullied me and for anyone that was being bullied. My life had changed. I no longer feared being bullied.

By the age of twenty-six I had reached a weight of around 330 pounds or 150 kilos and was strong enough to lift any average person over my head. The mind, once it is focused on finding a solution, will do its utmost to fulfill its needs and wants.

Some years ago a friend invited me to a dinner, where as a surprise he introduced me to another boy from the same school I had attended but who was in the year below mine. He reminded me that I had become the protector of the weak and the minorities. It seems I had taken over the school and much of the bullying came to a stop.

The degree of fear that I had created around me by my ever-growing size and strength solved my problems and, I believe, in many ways saved my life.

"Destiny is not a matter of chance; but a matter of choice. It is not a thing to be waited for; it is a thing to be achieved."

William Jennings Bryan

Chapter 2

Change Directions is a book about the challenges faced by those who seek change. It sets out to give clarity and inform individuals who seek to understand the difficulties that often bring frustration and confusion to the process of creating change.

It is not intended to give directions on how to live your life, after all, that is your prerogative. It is about showing how to give your mind directions in the event that you desire to have change.

Much of the book is written to give some insight to the practical difficulties we face when we seek change and the elements that stop us from directing our mind toward what we want.

Change Directions also describes some of the more common thinking errors that we maintain in our thinking and attitudes.

At this juncture, it may be prudent to point out that there is a strong possibility you will be distracted from reading your book. There is already a possibility that your mind will look to find ways for you to avoid the information contained. Just be aware and vigilant as this distraction can occur in the most unexpected ways.

You might misplace this book or find ways of putting off getting to grips with the content. Some people might believe that they know what it is all about and defend their position with a degree of arrogance.

This is all quite natural, yet it can be a little confusing. On one hand we want things to change, and on the other we mostly avoid it like the plague. For many, change is someplace in the future.

It is up to you from this point on. The compass is in your hands, and you decide where you want to direct your attention.

The first section of this book deals with some of the mechanisms that restrict change. The second part of the book gives clear directions on how to design and implement change. The process requires a time commitment to maximize the benefit.

It is possible to benefit just by reading *Change Directions* and not engaging in the process. The information will help you better grasp the process, and you will gain a deeper understanding and be better placed to act according to your needs and wants.

Change Directions is meant to be provocative and challenging. Its scope is to provoke movement in your thinking around the area of change.

It gives clear directions and examples of how to design change and what to consider when planning your future needs and wants.

My objective is to bring your awareness toward the mental process for change and to provide a toolkit to direct that change.

Chapter 3

To have change, we must know what we need and want to change and then, most importantly, what we want it to change to. Knowing that we are not happy with an element of our environment, behavior, personality, relationships, etc., is a good thing, but it is unlikely to alter much. We need a little more than that.

By directing your mind and taking some simple steps towards designing a new way forward, you can effect change.

Where we seek major change, we must be prepared to let go of what we know in order to reach the outcome we seek. For a while, this may cause a degree of anxiety or, possibly, excitement.

Those who are in the "change game" know that aiming towards something and then heading toward that something is the precondition to changing anything.

The most common action is to focus and analyze the situation then seeking to find the cause. We are naturally capable of analyzing and making a judgment of situations; it is as natural to us as breathing.

Analysis and judgment for some can become an obsessive pastime with no valuable purpose other than perhaps to validate and distract. Caution is necessary, as overanalyzing can cause the prolonging of pain unnecessarily.

There are times when it is essential to understand how something is doing what it is doing. If a mechanism is not doing what we expect it to do, then it makes sense to understand what and how this is happening. We can then look to correct the situation by seeking better solutions.

Seeking cause is very natural to us. The mental operating system was designed to do this. The critical factor here is the point at which we actively seek a solution. This is accomplished by designing a way forward and then taking action. Only when we seek a solution will one be found. This seems logical and obvious, yet many people struggle with this simple reality.

"You can analyse the past but you have to design the future."

Edward de Bono

It seems so obvious, yet we are blinded by its obviousness. Any rational reasoned person will tell you that you need to know where you are going to stand a chance of getting there.

We tend to be good at finding solutions when it comes to machinery and situations where we are not so emotionally attached. We are also engaging where the accountability for that change is not placed upon us. For example, if we were asked to reorganize the office, we would more likely engage with that process because it was an instruction.

If it is something outside of us, it may be easier to engage in the change. Certainly, we are great at telling and showing others a better way and even show signs of disbelief when they do not take our advice.

When it comes to changing our own environments, relationships, behavior's, attitudes and the like, it becomes somewhat more difficult. We are resistant to explore areas that could result in having more pleasurable experiences in life.

There are many books and other aids that help people to be empowered by having the right tools to change. There are workshops run by "great shepherds" that inspire, motivate and sometimes even provide enlightenment and sufficient insight to inspire change.

Many have great skill sets and are employing these skills in helping themselves and others to a degree towards creating changes.

It seems to me, however, that there is a shortfall between the energy we invest in learning and training and the degree of change achieved. Some people need to exert great discipline to apply themselves to accomplish change. Yet once we understand the concept of change, it can become effortless.

Chapter 4

Change is the ending of one process or action and the beginning of another. It sounds easy when described with words, but it is not so easy to take action when it comes to creating a significant change.

Most people would agree that they are seeking to improve the quality of their lives. Yet so many people living with discomfort stay stuck, unable to create a shift from their current situation, and so their discomfort becomes normality.

Change needs to be sought, encouraged, directed and commanded. Change is different, something that was once one way, changing and transforming to become something else, something new, something different and, all being well, something better.

Perhaps you think that you can change your circumstances by simply saying you do not like or want what is happening.

Or maybe you believe that if your partner, boss, parent, or friend changed then you would be happy. All too often the expectation is that others need to make the change.

The reality is that we are all getting what we believe we will get. We are experiencing what our minds know and have accepted. To think that we deserve better is not enough to create change. To hope or wish that things could be different is not enough.

If it were so easy, we would all use that method. We often talk about wanting things to be different yet struggle to realize that the difference we seek needs to be of our own making, and ultimately, of our own creation.

Chapter 5

We have discussed that we must make change occur in our own lives. But there is another way in which change occurs when events around us change our circumstances to which we are forced to adapt. This is an enforced change and, to a large degree, out of our control.

Say you use your checkbook to pay for goods. One day you discover that checks are no longer accepted by the local shop. Now you are forced to find an alternative way of paying. You may need to consider using a credit card.

Oddly enough, because we so much resist making change happen, we tend to become accustomed to enforced change. Somehow, we just adapt to everything that is changing around us without giving it much thought. We just go with the general flow with the occasional grunt.

We can easily be programmed externally to adjust our behavior. Just looking at car travel highlights how our travel experience and behavior has changed. We have accepted the onslaught of cameras, speed bumps, complex road marking, parking restrictions, payments, electronic parking payment and penalty methods and we have adapted to them.

The mind adapts to almost anything it is faced with. We continue until faced with the next enforced change. This is an important point to remember.

Unfortunately, few of us have grabbed the hand of the puppeteer and taken the control available to us. Now you can create a new destiny and you can decide which direction your life takes.

We might be in a place of work that is not stimulating yet may stay there until the company decides to relocate or close. Redundancy is forced upon us, and the next thing we know is that we are seeking new employment. Change has occurred through someone else's actions or circumstances.

Change is about directing our attention towards having a different experience, and in order to have that, we need to head in a new direction. If you keep doing what you have always done, you will most likely keep getting what you have always got.

Instead, we must aim at something purposefully, having an outcome in mind that takes us to what benefits us directly or indirectly. We must know our objective and set a goal towards it or choose to be somewhere different.

Seeking out options and then choosing the one best for us, as well as creating opportunities where choices are thin on the ground, is the objective of clear-minded individuals who have a zest for life and therefore experience a sense of contentment.

The talent is in the choices.

There are numerous reasons and considerations to contemplate before we engage with the process for change. Some of these reasons can seriously change the course of our life's experiences, and others can be as simple as choosing a new brand of toothpaste.

What is important to grasp about change is that it continues to occur with or without our directing it. Change has always been inevitable and will continue to be so long after we have departed. It is perhaps the surest thing in life.

It is useful to participate in designing a way forward that enhances the quality of our experiences.

"Man sooner or later discovers that he is the master-gardener of his soul, the director of his life."

James Allen

Chapter 6

At this point I would like to bring up a particular objection of some people, suggesting that if something is not broken, why fix it? This position implies that progress is best left alone.

However, if that were so, civilization would not have evolved past the point of our basic needs being met. We would still be travelling on foot and cooking on open fires. We would be unable to cure ourselves of most serious ailments.

I know you get the point; progress, like change, is essential and inevitable.

Why wait for something to break to see if we can make improvements? If something can be improved or made better, it makes sense to find the way to create that improvement.

Things are changing all the time, and what was once great could now be obsolete. We need to be attentive to life in ways that perhaps we are not educated to be.

Additionally, change is minimized by perpetuating a process. By continuing to think or do something in a particular way, we are ensuring its historical continuity. We become resistant to change whilst complaining that things are not good.

Concepts like tradition, custom, duty, etc., ensure that we maintain a process sometimes long after it serves us. We are trapped by this and discouraged from seeking to change it.

There are many reasons that historical continuity is such an obstacle to change. I suggest that fear is a natural resistance to change. We are discouraged to change things. It is all about keeping something recognizable, identifiable, and predictable. That is what the mind seeks and finds.

Few of us dare to step out of the known and recognized map of our reality. It is as if the idea of searching beyond the known territory is taboo.

The risk of change for those of us who know a process very well is also great. We may not be able to cope with changing it, as it could weaken us. Consequently, we tend to defend its need wherever challenged.

The objective is to keep things as they are and simply shore up the cracks as they occur - the sticky plaster approach to fixing most anything and everything. We are to a greater or lesser degree fearful of change in many areas of our lives.

However, there are numerous mind tools available that allow us to explore and evaluate situations to overcome our resistance and make improvements both in our professional and personal lives.

The reasons for this resistance are rarely explored, yet once understood they can bring great insight and enlightenment and provide a catalyst for change.

Setting new directions need not be so frightening. In fact, it can be so liberating that you may wonder what took you so long.

In some instances, we will wait to become skilled at change before we engage in a new process. It is like waiting to become an expert at riding bicycles before we get on and ride. No progress was ever made by a turtle that did not stick its neck out.

There is, of course, another important perspective to consider. The action taken by choosing to stay on the merry-go-round is also risky. There is a risk in doing and a risk in not doing.

In some cases, we can set ourselves up by believing that because we have selected a way of thinking about the world we have to defend it. Even though circumstances may have changed, the defense of our perspective continues.

We can also get very good at defending this perspective, to the point of becoming expert at it. Once we have become an expert, we are likely to become even better at defending our rightness. For us it is easier to defend our view than explore unknown territories.

We can all be trapped by our own intelligence.

This can sometimes be seen in cases of those who display an air of arrogance or grandiosity. In fact, anyone who avoids exploring and questioning their own understanding is trapped by their fear of perhaps having to adapt and change.

In some cases, we can become worn down by the struggle to understand how we got to be where we are. The energy used to process what is happening and to have our needs and wants met is forgone, quashed through exhaustion and we simply run out of steam.

Complacency can creep in undetected, and before we know it we become just part of the scenery and the problem. We are affected by the circumstances that govern us. By letting our awareness become hazy, we lose control, and with it the ability to direct our lives; a little here, a little there, and we suddenly realize that we are in a place that resembles quicksand.

Some of us have a tendency to shy away from the internal conflict of embarrassment to avoid change. To instigate change can be painful just in case we are challenged and have to account for our actions.

Similarly for those of us who have a propensity for feeling guilty, change can be a huge mountain to climb. Guilt has a tendency to keep us moving only to the degree that we believe others find acceptable.

"The cloying sweetness of approval spoils our taste for personal power".

Anne Dickson

It seems that other people's views and opinions are more important than our own happiness. Even if it is not in our best interest, we tend to value the comments of others for fear of upsetting the relationship or at worst being rejected.

Perhaps the most common reason for the lack of progress in our personal and professional life is the lack of awareness of our current position. Something that we are not conscious of is the energy being consumed to keep us where we are. The cost of awareness is high and needs to be considered.

To be constructively aware of ourselves is energy consuming, yet without awareness we are unconscious of what is happening and left to experience the effects as they happen to us.

Chapter 7

It helps to focus the mind if the mind knows what it is looking for. When you know what your desired outcome is and why you need and want it, it is much easier to know and understand you have it when you have reached it. To do this you must be aware of what is happening around you.

Awareness requires a great deal of energy. To be in the here and now is like a full-time job that requires diligence and correct persistence. The mind is more focused and responsive when it knows what it is looking for.

Awareness does not happen unless you give your attention to it. To be aware, we are required to be present in the here and now.

There has been increased interest in books that refer to being in the here and now. Something that I would encourage you to do is be aware, be here and be now, as best you can.

However, with the amount of activities we participate in daily, it is difficult for the mind to maintain constant awareness. Our mind is designed to create habits, patterns and routines. Automation has pride of place in the cosmos of our minds.

It is prudent to project into the future for important matters. You will need to consider the future consequences of the action or inaction of today's decisions.

The mind is not designed to be permanently switched on and processing. It is restricted by the degree of energy it has available. Like a muscle, it tires and needs nutrition and rest.

So, the mind needs to automate as many processes as possible. The mind creates repeatable patterns to cope with routines. This makes it, and therefore us, more efficient and increases our chances of survival.

Where it experiences an unknown situation, the mind seeks to understand it and to create a response that it can utilize in the future. Where it has a ready-made response, it will use it and save the energy of having to work it out.

The mind needs to be alert to deal with threats or opportunities. The rest of the time, it is on autopilot.

The mind is a self organizing, pattern making and self actualizing mechanism. Once it recognizes a situation, it responds according to what it knows. Recognition occurs through perception.

The way we identify and recognize anything is perception.

The challenge here is to find ways of perceiving things in a way that will most benefit us. This requires our awareness to be focused on interpreting things clearly and constructively.

Many people struggle with awareness, and I believe that this is one of the most challenging aspects for our mind to overcome. Like a magnet travelling through a tray of metal filings, the mind needs to avoid picking up too many filings if it is to endure the journey.

To the mind, filings are opinions. Each time we have an opinion we are attaching ourselves to something that requires processing. Opinions tend to be based on past experiences. That may not help us make an informed decision about a future action.

Remember that every time we process anything it costs energy as it requires our attention. This can consume a great deal of our resources and can unnecessarily distract us from our needs and wants.

The degree of attachment to what is going on around and within us determines the energy consumption. Passionate people tend to consume a great deal of energy.

Energy conservation requires that we do not have an opinion on anything we do not *have* to have an opinion on.

Reserving opinions to things that affect our needs and wants requires diligence and correct persistence. That is not to say that we do not have an opinion on our football team's performance or how great the dinner is, just that we need to control where we invest our energy and ensure we have enough to get our needs and wants met.

Energy can be increased through diet, physical exercise, simplifying perspectives and clear thinking processes. What doesn't help is tension, anxiety, worry, fear and frustration. Additionally, some medications can deplete energy and distort our perception.

By not being aware we are trapped and unable to step off life's merry-go-round long enough to see that life is still what we thought it was when we got on. Some would prefer to leave their blinkers on and just hope that things will turn out ok.

Paying attention to our degree of fulfillment, being aware of our aspirations, and exploring if there is better to be had is critical to change; it may be that all is well and that we may simply seek different experiences.

We need to observe and notice if we are in time with our ever-changing world and our relationship to it whilst remaining curious and wondrous about what it has to offer.

Evaluating our experiences is personal, so seek and select what is best for you. Other people's opinions may contribute to our evaluation, but ultimately it is our decision and needs to serve our greater good.

To help with the evaluation process, many books and methods encourage ways of changing. There are simple methods such as the SMART set, where we are asked to consider the acronym in set stages: S for specific, M for measurable, A for attainable, R for realistic, and T for time bound.

These have their uses, though I would offer that they leave gaps that require more detail. Nonetheless, they are a great reminder of what it's about.

Our focus needs to be clear and our attention firmly fixed on the task of selecting an area of our lives to change. Then we design a way forward towards our desired outcome. Our needs and wants must be served.

Focusing on the various aspects of our lives requires that we simply explore from a place of curiosity. What would work better if we could change it? There is a risk here of getting lost in possibilities. Too many options can cause confusion and procrastination.

There can be a degree of fear when we want change yet do not want to lose or give anything up. We might consider the effects on others and find ourselves forgoing change and quit seeking so as not to upset them.

We can be and are often bullied by opportunities. For some of us the options may be too many and varied. This could result in becoming stuck or trapped by choice.

Not doing anything is a choice.

Energy is easily dissipated when we allow ourselves the luxury of indecision and self-doubt. Indecision steals our time. Indecision is sometimes the cause of the cause of catastrophe.

Selecting the best option available and disregarding all other options whilst engaged in the change process requires willfulness and correct persistence for our attention to remain focused.

Constructing the desired outcome requires thoughtful diligence, and time needs to be set aside for this process. It may seem that just because we have formed the idea in our minds that the goal has been set.

The second part of this book is dedicated to helping you with this element of the change process. It is a step-by-step process designed to give clarity and a better understanding of what we seek.

Chapter 8

There have not been many books written on the subject of setting goals, objectives, and well-formed outcomes. Most books are geared around being positive and having a winning outlook and some detail surrounding your desired outcome. Why is that not enough?

Whilst these books add value, knowledge and improve our general understanding, they do lack a *certain something*.

That *certain something* is a clarity that I believe *is* the difference that makes the difference. It is an understanding of the change process through developing a better personal relationship with the mechanism that motivates our mind to change.

Our tendency is to amble along hoping, wishing, praying and sometimes manipulating, forcing, threatening and scaring ourselves toward getting something we believe we want.

In the reality of the mind the process is simple. Decide where you want to get to and get going. Yet if it is that simple, why is it that so many people are left stuck and unfulfilled? Simple does not necessarily mean effortless or without fear.

There are those who are paralyzed with guilt or a sense of duty. Others may fear disappointment or believe themselves unworthy of getting more out of life. For those it is not easy to change through seeking improvement, as it could further fuel their lack of worth.

In some instances the tendency is to want more and conceal it, just in case your family or friends see you wanting more and think of you as ungrateful, dissatisfied, above them, etc., fuelling feelings of guilt.

The probability is that most people do not seek change with any conviction, often changing their minds about what to change or continuing with the uncertainty of what change could bring.

The tendency is to amble along and hope that we will survive somehow and that things will become better. Like a lottery, occasionally someone wins.

Often it is not so much that people do not aspire to want more but rather that they do not understand how the mind operates. This results in setting ill-formed goals which manifest undesirable outcomes.

There tends to be a lack of understanding in what the mind strives to obtain by default; that is to say, the mind reverts to doing what it has always done and thus maintains the status quo.

Let us be very clear about this next point. There is always a default goal at play. If we think that we have not directed our minds in any particular direction, we are mistaken. We have past patterns of experience that our mind replays repeatedly until we direct it elsewhere.

If what we know is to be sad and we have not made a decision to experience something else, then our mind will take us to situations that create sadness. This is what it knows, and that is what it will do. It is an unspecified goal that will continue until we decide to experience life differently.

Wherever your focus is placed, your mind follows, and that most likely is where you will end up.

Remember that your mindset is also the director of your outcome. The attitude you adopt in itself is an indicator to your mind of what experience is to be had.

You may feel as though you are going round in circles. That is the goal. Not staying focused on your goal is as if you're shooting at a moving target, something the mind is not good at doing. Moving targets stress the mechanism. A hit-and-miss situation is certainly uncertain.

In some ways we could consider that within us, there is an aversion to the process of getting something new. A part of us simply keeps on expecting the same. The known and the predictable have a compelling appeal to the mind and satisfy the needs of security, stability and certainty.

The mind needs to be instructed only when things are required to be done differently. Otherwise, the mind utilizes its existing coping strategies to deal with everyday events in the way that it has coped with them in the past. It uses its cached and learnt experiences to deal with current, upcoming and future needs.

> "We look at the present through a rear-view mirror.
> We march backwards into the future."
>
> Marshall McLuhan
> (The Medium Is the Massage 1967)

It can be a little difficult to grasp that the mind is actually indifferent to the reality that it lives in on one important condition the reality we live in must be safe. By safe, I am talking about stable, predictable and known.

Outside of stability, the mind simply experiences the life it has become accustomed to. It follows the directions given through action and attitude, and when not engaged in that process it is using its past experiences to keep safe.

This precondition creates a challenge for those seeking change. The mind needs stability first and foremost. The idea of things changing can cause an internal conflict experienced as mild anxiety at one end of the scale to terror at the other.

A change of job for some gives cause for a low level of anxiety, whereas a divorce could present a high degree of fear. An important point to understand is that it is usually the *thought* of that change which enables immobilizing emotions and not the *act* of change itself.

Change is instant.
What can take time is reaching a decision to change.

Keep in mind that the mind is focused on keeping things stable, and if it is to engage in change it needs to stabilize the situation as quickly as possible. Therefore, our mind will always seek to stabilize any unstable situation much like water rebalancing itself after a storm.

There is an extraordinary ability that the mind has. This ability exists in most humans and is one that allowed us to survive global epidemics and other catastrophes; we are able to adapt to virtually any situation that is forced unexpectedly upon us.

The idea of migrating for some might seem inconceivable. Moving to another country where everything from the culture to the language and rules are different can seem unthinkable. Yet many millions accomplish this every year.

Many disasters and misfortunes that have occurred in the past seemed insurmountable. Yet looking backwards, we have somehow overcome and survived. We adapted and conquered. Adaptation is an inherent feature in humans.

Chapter 9

The driving force behind our actions comes from one of two basic instincts. These basic instincts are pain or pleasure. Either we are seeking to get away from painful experiences or we are heading towards a pleasurable experience.

If our system can cope with the degree of pain it is experiencing then it does not actively seek to change. We can be in a difficult situation yet do little to change it. This includes our ability to cope with boredom, an important point that I will come back to later on in the book.

Spending too much time dwelling on why you don't want what you are getting takes you no closer to getting what you want. If anything, it perpetuates your belief and encourages more of the same.

When focus is placed on the negative experiences, the mind takes that as direction and it becomes the center of our focus. Think through your thoughts and ensure you stay focused on areas that enhance your experience of life.

It is practically useful to understand what the consequences of experiences have had on your belief system, how you adapted, and what you did thereafter to cope. (see Gold Counselling in the book list at the back of this book).

Change Directions is more concerned on where you want to go, not so much on where you have been. The focus is paramount if you are to change direction in some areas of your life.

For some of us it takes the fear of pain or punishment to create a drive for change. Generally, it matters not where we head so long as the threat is distanced.

All too often, we leave one painful situation only to find ourselves embroiled in another. Our mind continues to repeat what it knows, for it can only live through experience. No experience, no life.

There is a tendency to wish that things would be different but not to engage in the process of setting new directions. The familiar "I wish things were different" or "I wish I could" types of statements would suggest that the situation is not uncomfortable enough for a new direction to be set.

Often those in the "wishing game" are very able to evidence a case for not being able to do anything about their predicament. Analysis of the situation is bound to find a perspective to suit the individual.

> "Great minds have purposes;
> others have wishes."

> Washington Irving

Wishing suggests that things will somehow miraculously change, as if it is enough just to wish for it. It is as effective as a child wishing that his or her parents would stop arguing. I have not known that to work.

Unfortunately, mostly people choose to change only when their current situation is intolerable. In other words, things have to be unbearably painful before a new direction is sought.

Perhaps you need to hear rumors that a job you thought you were in line for is going to another colleague. This then spurs you into action to secure your needs and wants.

In some instances when a union of two people is uncomfortable, it is only when one discovers that the other is having an affair that he or she kicks into action and begins to create change.

Certain industries are renowned for creating high levels of emotional pressure and stress. People will adapt and endure to attain their needs and wants. For some people the stress is the motivating factor; better to have a stressful experience than nothing at all.

There are a number of reasons for this; for example, the pain of boredom may be too much. It could be that they simply believe that that is just how life is. Therefore, where there is not enough stress, a situation is caused to create it.

Boredom is not to be underestimated in its ability to wreak havoc. The danger of boredom is that it can result in sudden irrational behaviors or thinking that can result in unwanted experiences.

This can leave individuals wondering how they got themselves into such a mess. The solution to one problem has, in this instance, created another.

Where we act out of boredom, we can find ourselves being propelled to escape by finding almost anything to do to stop the frustration that is experienced.

A distraction could take any number of forms: having an affair, gambling, overeating and drinking, shopping, just about anything to get out of the feeling of boredom and into a feeling of excitement.

The risk is great if boredom is left unchecked. The cure for boredom is curiosity. Develop the characteristic of curiosity as best you can. It could well revolutionize your way of thinking.

In contrast, it seems that many who are involved in meaningful activity are less prone to irrational behaviors.

The difficulty here is recognizing that the mechanism endures stress and anxiety for short bursts. Where it is under duress, the system begins to fail. We can be blind to the rising stress and find we are overwhelmed when the stress turns to distress.

The telltale signs are often missed because it all starts to feel as if it is normal to be like this. For some people the damage is irreversible. They experience burnout and can suffer permanent exhaustion, in some cases leading to chronic stress.

"A long habit of not thinking a thing wrong gives it a superficial appearance of being right."

Thomas Paine

That is precisely what can happen. Everything becomes normalized.

The cut-off point for most people is when the level reaches a critical factor where, if they continue, they could sustain damage. It appears that some are driven to change only when they have reached this point. For some it can be too little too late.

When faced with the inevitability of having to change, the mind adapts to the new situation it finds itself in. The speed of adaptation is dependent on the circumstances and the resources an individual has available at the time.

A person being made redundant at work can experience a trauma, especially if it comes unexpectedly. This can debilitate them for a while and leave them feeling hopeless, helpless and even worthless. In time, the situation stabilizes as they become accustomed to their new circumstances.

The force of change has enabled them to be free to change, and whether they choose to benefit from it or be hindered by it is the difference between choosing a destination or being a passenger to it.

This can often be found in relationships that people hang on to; the type of relationship that is painful and often found to be lacking pleasure or care, yet the individuals involved hang in there as if their lives depended on it. People involved in such a relationship cannot contemplate an alternative. It becomes the only thing they have to hang on to. They will not let it go easily.

From their perspective it appears that the lack of options allows no space to consider an alternative.

For example, it could be that both parties are unable to cope with rejection and are consequently unable to reject their partner. They are trapped by the situation and their ability to cope with it. The reasons for this are endless and I would need to write another book to explore the subject fully.

When a shift is made and the system is destabilized, it automatically adapts to the new circumstances; and once it finds predictability again, it has found stability.

Chapter 10

Knowing and understanding are not the same. You may know something yet not fully understand it. You might know what an engine does and not understand how it does it. You may know that 2 + 2 = 4, however, that does not mean you understand calculation. When we can answer why something is so, we have an understanding. Understanding underpins knowledge.

What we know is dependent on what we understand. The better we understand it the more we know it.

The better the mind understands why something is as it is, the more chance we have of successfully recognizing it. The degree of understanding we each require is variable. Some of us need to fully grasp the situation whilst others need a general flavor to proceed.

Perhaps the simplest way to define understanding and knowing is to think of understanding as the why, how, when, where, etc., the detail that underpins our knowing of something.

It is probable that you have in the past met with people who, when you tell them something important, say "I know". Yet, you had a sense that told you they did not grasp it, they did not understand what you where telling them. They did not grasp the full meaning of your communications.

That is not to say that some people do not charge forth blindly and sail by the seat of their pants. It seems that for some, the less they know the better. They deal with issues as they arise.

This approach tends to be more so for the impetuous type. Often seen in our youth and evidenced in adults who have little regard of the consequences, little consideration is given to the outcome should it fail; they just shake it off and move on. That is fine, so long as they can recover from their failed experience.

Some people need to hit rock bottom or have a near death experience before they decide to change direction. They deal with enforced change on a need-to-change basis. They wait for something to happen in order to step into action only as the need arises.

This also includes people who are stuck in the ease of their life and circumstances. It's so easy to carry on doing what they have always done. At times, they can struggle with the repetitiveness. It is only when they reach an unacceptable degree of pain or where the situation stops them from continuing that they change direction for something new.

The trapped tend to be those people who have their biological and physical needs met. They tend to experience a degree of safety in their environment and have a family or extended family, perhaps a lover, and a sense of belonging socially. They are trapped by the lack of aspirations. There is no drive to want more so long as their basic needs are met.

It seems that if we find ourselves in a safe environment we can be trapped by it. Once an environment has been stabilized and accepted, it can be difficult to escape its stability. Stability can be very addictive.

It helps to drive the mechanism for change enormously, when the mind understands the target especially where the target is desired. That is not to say that the mind cannot be coaxed or pushed into change, rather that it can be more certain of the desired outcome when it understands the place it needs to get to.

If you wanted to change careers to become a sales manager, it would be useful to know more than what the pay is and where you would be based. Understanding what is entailed would be prudent if you were to be successful at it.

The details of the position, the characteristics required, the type of qualification needed, the number of hours you would need to work, what would be expected of you, what the chances of progressing from there are, etc., all add to your resolve and help to minimize fear.

It's all about getting the details, the facts and the information that makes the knowing possible. Sometimes we look back at how we accomplished something and realize that if we had known what we had to go through to get there we might never have started the journey, or if we had known certain facts, we might have done it differently.

Our mind needs clear and direct instructions to where it needs to get to for a better chance of getting there. Our mind does not know what it does not know, so how can it take us to a place that it does not recognize? If you cannot recognize the place, it does not yet exist.

Often we find ourselves arriving somewhere that we may not have chosen; a job; a relationship; business we thought we were going to get, turns out not to be what we thought it was going to be.

What we thought it was going to be and what it turned out to be are two different places. Where we arrived is where our mind understood we needed to arrive and not necessarily where we imagined.

Our mind will take us to where it knows; it cannot take us somewhere it does not understand or recognize. Be clear about this, because if your mind doesn't recognize and understand that that place exists, it cannot take you there. It will continue to take you to what it knows and what it understands you mean.

For example, often people seeking to be in a relationship find themselves in relationships that are extraordinarily similar to the relationships they experienced in their formative years.

This is what the mind recognizes a relationship to be. It is unlikely to create something that does not resemble anything it can identify.

Chapter 11

One way we learn is by modeling: copying people's behaviors and characteristics. Relationships we witnessed and experienced with parents, siblings, friends, etc., are all observed and copied. That is how the mind learns and understands a relationship to be.

Mostly this is done unconsciously, though you may recall holding a hairbrush and looking in the mirror whilst pretending to be a rock star, or pretending to be a footballer scoring a goal. You might even notice the use of similar words, tones and looks of parents and others who were an influence in the past in your everyday life.

It is little wonder that when we find ourselves in a relationship we are likely to be replicating something from our past. It is, after all, what we know. So unless something specific is sought, we can expect a representation of what we know to manifest.

When an unspecific instruction is given, the mind seeks to find the closest understanding that it has to fulfill that instruction. It looks for a past experience as a reference to emulate.

When we set out to be in a relationship, the mind identifies our request based on what it understands a relationship to be. The obvious question is where the mind got the information that led to its understanding of what a relationship is in the first place.

Ambiguity is often at the heart of our goal's misfortune. Lack of clarity can cause years of frustration and misfortune. By simply not being clear or mumbling our goals, we could be perpetuating further frustration.

Sometimes we are unaware that our thoughts, which behave like magic magnets, attract emotional and physical experience. If the thoughts are laced around being a victim, the poor-me syndrome, then we are transmitting this to our own mind as something to strive for.

It could also be that this was a goal. To be a victim, our mind might be running a program that says "never be fulfilled". Perhaps in the past a "thought goal" was born from having things taken away from us. It could be that we were accused of never being satisfied. The possibilities here are endless.

I recall working with people who came to a decision that concluded "never be happy because when I am it is taken from me". These individuals are in a lose-lose situation. That *is* their choice based on what they believe is available to them.

On one hand their life is devoid of the benefits that an experience of being with someone would give them. Empty or at best shallow, it leaves them longing for more; on the other hand they will not attach to any cause of goodness in the event that they may lose it and are left empty and longing again.

Consider that many people live and die without ever revealing their thoughts, emotions, needs and wants. The fear of being open to the world, of being transparent, results in those individuals missing out on interacting with others at a level that allows reflection and growth.

I remember some years back a multimillionaire came to see me because he was not coping with the stresses of life. We did some work around motives, outcomes and beliefs to enable him to understand. He said that although he had four million, he knew that if he reached five million things would be less worrisome.

The statement left me wondering, and so I asked him if he had stopped to consider if the same thought had been there when he was going for the first million.

To his amazement he realized that the outcome for him was not that he was seeking to have millions, though he did enjoy it; it was to not get bored. He feared complacency and just kept giving himself higher targets to keep the pressure on himself.

If it were not for the fact that he was killing himself, I would have told him to enjoy his journey. But that stress caused him tension in his relationship, sleeplessness, hair loss, etc.

When a goal has been met, the mind needs to know to stop seeking it. This can be accomplished by accepting through acknowledgment and appreciation that the goal has been met. Then a new goal needs to be set.

Let's say that you have set your mind a goal to establish a new relationship. At the point at which you accept a relationship, the mind stops seeking it even though you may not necessarily have found someone to match your needs and wants. Because you have accepted it, as far as your mind is concerned, it has accomplished the goal.

By accepting a situation, you have stopped your mind seeking further. Happy or not, the goal as it has been understood has been delivered.

I recall a person who thought, no matter who was in their life, "How do I know there is not someone out there better for me?"

Accepting a goal simply requires that we stop looking at other possibilities. Once we accept a situation, we accept that our objective has been fulfilled.

Uncertainty can leave us wondering if this is the right person for us, which some interpret as an inability to commit. This sends a signal to the mind that the goal has yet to be reached and to continue looking and making possibilities more obvious.

For some no matter what goals they set, once reached they doubt they have reached their goal and do not accept it just in case there is better out there. This is often borne from confusion, ambiguity, self-doubt or perhaps a need never to be satisfied.

It could also be that the underlying goal is to wander through life dipping in and out of many relationships. Once a particular act has been accomplished, it's over and we move on to the next objective.

Therefore, the ability to set a goal that has value, know you have it, revel in it and satisfy your needs and wants whilst setting future goals is priceless.

Just as you might use a map to help you get someplace you haven't been before, the mind needs instruction and engagement with the process. Getting in a car with a map is part of the activation process but not the journey or the destination.

Most people we meet want more out of life; not a bad thing. After all there is plenty available for all. But in order to have some things we may need to let other things go.

Now that's not always so easy. For some people it can be painful even to contemplate. Just the idea of ending something causes anxiety for most people.

Endings can bring with them a degree of uncertainty and instability, the very thing the mind seeks to avoid. It also brings us closer to the greatest fear of all, loss.

Obviously not all losses are painful; in some instances we welcome the ending of something. It may bring with it great relief. The end of a difficult contract or a turbulent relationship brings with it a degree of relief.

Loss is such an integral part of our life, yet we do our utmost to avoid it. It is inevitable that it will occur; still we fear it to the point that many will seek never to experience pleasure for fear of losing it.

When something comes to an end it is often not seen as a good thing during its ending. The probability is that pain is experienced and new ways will have to be found to cope.

This is part of the coping mechanism and operating system of the mind. Change inevitably means letting go of something. Reality, as we know it, is going to change to some degree if we move to a better place. Ultimately a new stability will be found.

Here we are talking about the greatest fear that befalls humanity; the fear of loss is experienced as pain in most endings, the pain of detaching from something or someone we have attached to.

"Some people think you are strong when you hold on. Others think it is when you let go."

Sylvia Robinson

When we are settings goals we need to be clear that in striving for that goal something will come to an end. The world we have become accustomed to will change.

Some people I have assisted who have endured a fraught and abusive childhood have suggested that it would have been better if their parents had separated and gone their own way, whilst others wished that things could have stayed the same.

Most parents have suggested that their reason for staying was "for the kid's sake". I don't know about that, as I do not know any children who have appreciated their parents staying together for them.

To avoid the fear that loss brings, the mind will do whatever it needs to do. In its quest it can be, and often is, very divisive.

The choice is to accept or reject changes based on the merits of the possibilities, which need to include gains as well as losses. We are naturally focused on the losses and need to apply our attention to gains when designing change.

Chapter 12

Change is inevitable, and with it comes the need to adapt to our environment. Often we are unaware that change is occurring, and the adjustments are such that we seem to cope with them.

"It is not the strongest of the species that survive, nor the most intelligent, but the one most responsive to change."

Charles Darwin

If you have been someplace long enough to become accustomed to it, then leave and return some years later you tend to notice the changes that have occurred. Yet someone who lives a life there is unlikely to notice the changes occurring. Change seems to happen at a pace that generally keeps us unaware of the transformation.

When setting goals, we need to look at the big picture and accept that change will bring with it a new stability. Be assured that the mind will use every resource to accomplish stability.

The anxiety that we are likely to experience is part of the change process. If I suggest that you can have what you want, so long as you understand it and know the implications of having it, then what would stop you from going for it if you have the resources to get it?

Fear plays its part in goal setting. Not wanting to shatter an illusion is often a contributing factor to avoiding change. Some people would rather live a life in fantasy than explore the possibility of getting their goal and experiencing it in reality.

I believe that many of us obtain the satisfaction of accomplishing our goals in the safe and perhaps heightened imaginary world. This is the safe environment that allows the mind to experience without the need to change anything.

Many of us would rather read about someone else's exploits in the safe environment of our homes than explore developing a life that allows us to experience it firsthand.

Romance novels and other similar books are often at the top of peoples reading preferences. I would hazard a guess that if someone is reading a romantic novel, romance is lacking in their life. Why else would they be reading book after book on the subject of romance?

Let's take a person who daydreams, whilst sitting in the box room of an office block with a feeling of satisfaction, of how they would run the business differently. Whilst enjoying having all the books on leadership, time management and strategic planning around them they are pretending to themselves that they are running the company. This experience gives them a feeling of accomplishment through allowing themselves to believe in a grandiose way that they could do better whilst doing nothing about it.

This person is highly unlikely to ever make the move to becoming the person they dream of being. The solution for this individual is to put the books away and face reality, and take the necessary steps needed to fulfill their potential.

There is a greater chance for a woman who gives her pets human names and who pampers, cuddles and treats them like children even to the point of calling them "my babies" not becoming a mother than one that accepts them as a pet.

In a similar way a woman collecting a family of dolls and who refers to them as "my family" is highly unlikely to ever have one of her own in a pragmatic reality.

The world of fantasy reality, also known as hyperrealism, is where the mind has the experience of accomplishment in the safety of a mental framework. There is no connection to the evidence-based world of pragmatic reality.

The world of fantasy reality is perhaps as seductive as the world's most powerful drug. Be assured for those of you who are suffering with this that it is going to be one of the most challenging conditions to overcome in life. So much so that some of you will feel the withdrawal symptoms of an addict by the third day. The solution is to monitor when your mind seeks to lure you into this ever-available world of fantasy that is so cheap to create and powerful to resist.

A solution to cease being drawn into fantasy reality is when you find yourself starting to fantasize, stop and affirm to your mind in an adult tone, "*Not this way,*" and immediately shift your attention to something that is happening now.

A common reason for lack of drive towards setting goals is the possibility that we are getting more by imagining it. It is certainly less energy consuming for the mind to provide the experience in the safety of its domain. It certainly removes the possibility of losing it, and the risk of not getting it in pragmatic reality.

It is also useful to accept that it may not have been possible to reach a particular goal in the past. Just because it was not possible at that time does not mean that other goals are not possible.

People often pick safe goals that are a natural progression. For example, the supervisor who wants to become a manager; or a lorry driver who wants to be a driving instructor. These are, as far as the mind is concerned, less threatening job changes.

There are possibly those who make slow progress by incrementally improving their position. They tend to take small steps and strive for small changes rather than take a risk and experience some dramatic change. For some people this might work.

Most of us, however, have the capacity to accomplish some incredible feats with the help of our minds. Fear is the hurdle that needs to be overcome first if it rears its head. In some cases it might mean that the hurdles cannot be jumped, but they can be knocked over and you can still be victorious.

Perhaps you need to consider that the majority of goals set are likely to create a degree of fear. This fear is designed to alert us to the possibility that our stability will change and as a consequence we need to exert caution.

Fear may sometimes be interpreted as a signal to stop, when really it is principally a signal for danger. How we react to it is critical and vital to the success of any major changes we seek.

In my opinion it is important that we take notice of the "danger signal" in the most constructive way possible. Where we are alerted to the danger of change, we need to seek out more reasons for doing what we want to do. We need to minimize the chance of a negative outcome.

We need to truly understand our need for the change we seek. This substantially reduces the degree of fear we experience, perhaps to the degree that we simply stay alert and adaptable on our journey.

We need to perceive a greater value in what we are doing than for doing something else. It helps if you are able to get a "this feels right" kind of feeling. There is a strong chance that not only you appear to lack fear, you are riding a euphoric wave. You just know it's right.

Often setting goals is confused with planning. The detailing of an entire journey from beginning to end is not the same as a goal. There can be a few gaps in our perceived goal. It would be incorrect to believe that you need all the details in accomplishing the goal.

If you know the entire journey including the hurdles to jump and how to jump them, then it's not so much a goal as it is an action plan.

Chapter 13

Many who fail to set goals tend to believe that they are unlikely to reach them, so why bother? This requires serious reviewing if you are going to avoid being trapped by such a belief.

Beliefs play a significant role in achieving goals. What are the chances of getting into a great relationship if you believe such a relationship does not exist or that you are not worthy of it? Little, I think.

In some instances where you may have landed yourself a great catch, you can scuttle it by maintaining an attitude of disbelief that this has happened to you. Then you go on to justify the outcome appropriately and are back on the trail to find the "ideal suitor".

If you do not believe that something has happened and are unable to embrace it in your mind as a possibility, you are indirectly rejecting the offering and may go on to sabotage your good fortune to validate your disbelief.

A common feature of people who are likely not to accomplish their goals is to be very attached to the outcome. So much emotional energy is placed on *having* it that little is left for *getting* it.

In that case, only those who are obsessed with their goal and who can attach themselves to someone else who can get it for them might reach their goals. The price though may be a lot more than they might have imagined.

Additionally, just the act of *wishing* a goal to happen sends a message of doubt and in some cases desperation to the mind. Why would you be wishing for something that was inevitable unless you doubted it?

There are mixed messages being transmitted and received. Consider those who declare their needs and wants whilst praying for a miracle. The miracle is the mind's ability. As far as we are concerned, that is what the mind is designed to do. No miracles are required, just clear and concise directions without doubt and any degree of anxiety.

It is important to avoid giving mixed messages. Staying indifferent and disassociated whenever doubt rears its head is paramount. Learn to shrug off the negative thoughts. There are books available to help minimize the negative thought. I believe that it can be quite challenging to train the mind to cease having negative thought. Fortunately, it's only challenging, not impossible.

I might suggest that some mental retraining is required and propose a simple yet effective strategy on my Website www.change-directions.com for those that seek it.

Some believe that to set goals they need to know every step of the way; that it's all mapped out. They need to know, when, where, who, how, etc., before they can act.

It is not possible to know certain details, as some can only be gleaned en route or when the goal has been accomplished. The journey provides many things such as insight, inspiration, motivation, encouragement and unexpected rewards. This is, after all, life.

It's as if you are walking across a plank. It is important to stay focused to your target, and it is important that you start on the right foot and that it is definitely on the plank. After the first couple of steps, you really need to be looking at where you're going if you're going to make it.

You often see that those who make it to the other side seemed to glide across with their heads held high whist instinctively knowing where to step without looking.

There is a danger that if you're heading to a place that is occupied, that the result could be costly. Understanding this element may be important to some readers.

Settings goals that require someone being displaced virtually ensures the unlikelihood of the goal ever being reached. No two people can occupy the same space at the same time, nor can they own something synchronously.

With the exception of scientific and mathematical objectives, it is a misconception that goals need to be specifically specific. If anything, the degree of absolutes can be the cause of the goal not being reached. Imagine setting a goal to get someone's job in your office. This person may have no plans to leave their post.

Your mind would have to wait until that person is moving on and then actively position itself to accomplish the goal. You might need to wait years or even run out of time.

Some years ago a lady came to me for some help to understand why things just did not seem to work out for her.

She was well read on positivity, the importance of imagining your goal and affirmations to keep it alive.

Her desire was to be on television, and she had perceived herself having the position of a presenter. She had set her sights on getting the show that was occupied by another presenter. Needless to say she was not getting very far in her quest.

Not only was she not getting the opportunity to be assessed for a presenter's job, she also pointed out to me that she was exhausted in her attempts and could evidence this because she had more than two hundred rejection letters in a box.

Her goal was virtually impossible to accomplish. We worked through the issue and set a well-designed outcome into action. The letters destroyed, she set off in a new direction to fulfill her needs and wants.

Serendipity occurred within about two weeks when she noticed a newspaper had been left on the seat next to hers on the underground train. The page was open and folded at an advertisement seeking a lady to do a television program. She dismissed it as just a chance thing and moved on.

The next morning a friend of hers rang to ask if she had seen the advert, knowing that it was something she wanted to do.

With the outcome clarified and designed, a television opportunity arose; she accepted an opportunity to work on television and experienced the fulfillment of her needs and wants. She changed directions and evolved.

It is important to grasp that the mind just needs to understand what experience you require. Where exactly the experience comes from is not that important. If you have your desired outcome specified and the experience understood, your mind has a better chance of fulfilling your needs.

If you want to run a department in an office, does it really matter which department it is and for which division or company you work for, so long as you are enjoying the experience and it is taking you along the path you have chosen?

Job satisfaction has a lot to be said for it. When we consider that we spend so many years of our life working, we may as well set out to enjoy our work.

In some instances specific vagueness is needed and necessary. A bicycle chain needs to be linked and loosely connected so that the chain can find its way around the cogs and adapt to your requirements.

Rigidity is a sort of self-restraint that can easily become a stumbling block. If we are looking for a partner who looks exactly like someone we know, well, it's possible but not so easy.

The chances are more limited in pursuing such a goal than if we simply seek someone who made it possible for us to experience life beautifully. There are more of those kinds of people out there. I accept that a chemical connection also needs to exist.

In setting goals, certain aspects need to be vaguely specific whilst others need to be specifically vague.

You may want to be a successful lawyer; does it matter *where* you are being a successful lawyer? If it does, so be it; it may take a little longer. It may consume more of your resources and time to achieve your goal. It may not.

The talent is in the choices.

Chapter 14

Some goal-setting methods ask the question "with who do you want this goal?" as part of the goal setting process. When it comes to setting goals, the ones that are strictly personal are the ones less likely to falter.

You may be working in a department with several managers that may not share your common goal. They may be heading in another direction. They may have different and differing objectives.

So goals that incorporate other people tend to falter, as you can never be sure that what they are looking for in life is the same as what you seek. Where there is incongruence there is likely to be conflict.

A partner that wants the simple life may not make it too easy for the mind to fulfill your needs if you want travel and adventure. A conflict may arise from the mismatch of goals and desires. One could be inadvertently sabotaging the other's progress towards the needs being met.

When you consider this from a personal perspective, you may discover that you have goals that are in conflict with your partner's. There may be a conflict of interest. Your mind could be striving for something that conflicts at a level you may not recognize - unless, of course, you look for it. It may be prudent to be aware of this possibility before setting to change directions.

The solution is simple. Your goals, your needs and wants, your desires all need to be about you and for you. They need to be totally selfish. The principle benefactor needs to be you. If beyond that they go on to benefit others, then all the better. First, though, it needs to be you.

For groups, the dynamics are different and the process and method for pooling together resources for the common good is altered. For teams to work well together, the group dynamics need to fit. Often this process works better with a facilitator.

There is a common phenomenon that can be seen in people who are trapped by the ease of their situation. Imagine a person who knows their job inside out. No thinking is required because there is nothing to work out; they can do it with their eyes shut.

Aside from those who are happy and content with life, there is a group of people who are trapped by another type of problem: they have no problem that requires dealing with. For those of you who have studied Edward de Bono's work, you may recall "the no-problem problem."

It is subtle and luring and keeps people just so. It is just enough to fill their needs and wants. Un-happy; a place right in between happy and sad.

With such a simple, solid, easy routine, we can become so comfortably uncomfortable that it becomes difficult to make any great changes. We are not bored enough; the pain is insufficient to get us to shift a gear and have another experience or stretch our aspiration.

The tendency for those of us in this situation is to be blinded to better possibilities. We could be unable to see what else we could extract from our position at work. It could be that we cannot see value in striving for more based on what we are likely to get from the effort we are putting in.

It is also the stability that leaves us free of fear and devoid of anxiety. It can be a very addictive place to be. Everything is good on the basis that there is nothing bad happening.

It is understandable how motivation is often not enough to get us to act. It may be that we have to resort to causing instability in order to create movement. Rocking the boat is one option, which can be a little unpredictable as you never know who will fall out.

Sometimes it is enough to offer money, power or some other incentive to motivate an individual into action. The employee who passively goes along with whatever is going on is not easy to motivate in this way. There are no problems, so what's the problem?

Occasionally boredom sets in and frustration leaks out. Some people spend a little time in hyperrealism and imagine some experience and then return to stability. Others may have a short tantrum and let off a bit of steam then return to their reality.

A high degree of common sense is required when setting goals. Now, you are probably thinking that everyone has common sense.

Unfortunately that is not the case. I know many people who have common sense, yet I have not found anyone with enough of it. There always seems to be room for more.

Common sense can be seen as an ability that is acquired through childhood learning and development. Perhaps it's one of the things you can never have enough of.

In part, common sense is the ability to see things appropriately in context of the situation, whilst finding the most efficient and effective way to resolve it.

It would be short-sighted to set goals that lacked integrity. They could leave you feeling uncomfortable at best. When self-deception is present, that is when we are not acceptant of the situation as it really is, and the outcome is likely to be unfulfilling. It could be one sure way of never directing change with any degree of certainty. The deceiver is more often deceived.

Transparency is the cure, and the only way of assuring that is to give clear direct and specific instructions honestly.

I would like to further assist you by clarifying this important point. You are setting directions on your satellite navigation system to take you to a location. It knows where you need to go. If you deceive it by giving it the wrong starting point, the probability is that it will stay stuck in the position it's in or take you into the unknown.

It cannot make progress; it knows it is not where it is being told it is. It knows a different reality and will act on that basis. That is not to say that the mind cannot be duped temporarily.

In the long term, and especially with matters of the heart, the mind is to some degree aware of the reality of the situation.

Even when communication and direction is clear there is still the possibility that an error could be made in the interpretation. What we seek here is to minimize the possibility and maximize success.

Chapter 15

It is vital to know in advance that your goal is pragmatic and in keeping with your resources.

The last question in the questionnaire section requires that you validate your goal by asking a trusted and respected person to assess your goal. This is to ensure that the goal is not unrealistic.

An unrealistic goal could be wanting to be a coach for a Premier football team when you have had no training and are in your late eighties. I think you get the message.

Keeping the goal real is critical. Yet I have seen people set seemingly unbelievable goals that became reality. So it is worth always giving your mind a neural stretch.

Dare your mind to be remarkable; set out to do something outstanding that you might have thought improbable. It is useful to stretch your mind and is as beneficial as stretching your muscles enough to feel the benefit.

Much of this method is focused on ensuring that the goal is at best known and understood. This helps to minimize the fears that may be encountered on the journey to fulfilling needs and wants.

Suppose that you decide to live on your own. That's your goal, that's what you want and the idea appeals to you. There may be a degree of fear at how you will cope on your own.

By experiencing the goal in advance, you could realize that there is far less to fear. In this area we have an astonishing tool in the mind because we are able to pre-conceive an idea. Through our imagination we can test concepts to the degree we can create them in our minds.

Our imagination is our practice area. It is our test site. It is a place where there is privacy and latitude that enables us to explore possibilities. This is where we can explore the accomplishment of our goal whilst being safe in the knowledge that it is only a mental rehearsal.

It is unfortunate that most people of my generation have been weaned off of using their imagination. "Stop daydreaming, boy!" comes to mind.

Imagination is a critical component for change. The imagination area is useful to perceive possibilities, to test accomplishments and explore a number of hypothetical situations, places where we seek to find out what getting there will be like. Unlike hyperrealism, it is a place for exploring possibilities and getting a sense of being there.

Imagination is a place where we can look at things from multiple perspectives. In other words, what will change in my social life if I get this new position? What effect will it have on my family? What will happen to my relationship with my colleagues?

Spending a few minutes exploring the possibilities without being attached to anyone of them is of great benefit. It does bring a degree of peace to the anxiety that the unknown may create. Treat the experience as information gathering. It's temporarily pretending, a kind of internal role playing.

In the automotive industry, for example, when a new model of car is needed, it is first constructed with the aid of computers. It is tested on screen, the results are analyzed and if they are what is sought then construction of the design begins.

The objective is to minimize the negative influence of the unknown. The less left unknown to the mind, the less fear that is likely to be experienced.

The mind has another interesting twist when it comes to the unknown. On one hand it seeks to avoid it, and on the other, where curiosity is, it can become obsessed or compelled to know. The degree of curiosity determines the level of attachment to the object of our curiosity.

I would imagine that most of you reading this book have had moments of compelling curiosity that trapped you in a place you could not let go of until you knew the answer.

Where possible, be wondrous of what getting your goal will be like. Be curious; be intrigued as to how your mind will accomplish the goal for you.

You can wonder on the condition that you do not engage in predicting the detail. Prediction in this instance could be perceived as direction. You might discover that you have led your mind down a dead-end road. If you are predicting the path for your mind to follow, you had better have your facts right.

It is worthy of mention that when curiosity is employed, you will notice that in place of fear there will be a sense of awe as to how things turn out. This develops better abilities to change direction.

If you had to detail how you got to be where you are today, you would realize how hard it would be to explain all the things, people, and situations that you encountered that led you to where you are now.

To have designed the entire journey of your life from beginning to end is practically impossible.

Chapter 16

It's important to ease the mind's natural fear of the unknown by ensuring that you have a good understanding of where you want to go. The questionnaire later on in this book helps with this by provoking your mind.

The goals you set define in many ways who you are and what you're about. You can tell a lot about someone by what drives them and what they strive for in life.

You might want great things such as starting a charity and taking two to three years to have it established. Or you might be more into immediate thrills and book a parachute jump for next week. Neither is right nor wrong. These are just motivating factors.

This questionnaire is an opportunity to develop better quality goals, goals that are more fulfilling, longer lasting and perhaps even help others do better. It may be that you have fewer goals than others, yet far, far richer and more fulfilling results.

This is an opportunity to evaluate if you are getting enough out of life and review why you are doing what you are doing. By assessing the quality of your life you might decide to aspire for more. There is plenty to be had by all.

The consequences of this type of review could result in many better experiences and a sense of greater fulfillment. After all, if we are going to live a life we may as well enjoy the process and make it as extraordinary as possible.

The language you use on the questionnaire is also critical. Nothing is to be written in a negative context.

Example 1

"I don't want to be sitting in the office".

Example 2

"I don't want a partner who leaves his cups all over the place".

In the first example what the mind hears is where you do not want to be, but not where you *do* want to be. The mind is not too good at guessing where you need to be. So until it knows where you want to be, it will keep doing the familiar. Additionally, it turns the negative sentence into a negative action.

So be instructive and directive towards where you need to be. "I need to be working in an industry with an opportunity to be of help to people".

In the second example, the request leaves many possibilities of bringing someone into your life who is ultra tidy only to discover much later that they are obsessive at tidying up and insufferable about it.

Also consider what matters most to you. An example could be "I need and want a person who can respect and care for me and my needs".

Language is critical to ensure that there are minimal ambiguities. Some years back I co-authored a book that addresses some of these issues in communicating (you will find further details on *My Little Book of Verbal Antidotes* at the back of this book).

The big picture is crucial. Look at the outcome in a bigger context. It is important that when creating your goal there is no self-deception. Know why you are doing what you are doing. Be transparent with your reasons for inviting change into your life.

The key to this section is for you to understand the personal gain you will receive from doing this. Ask yourself, "What's in it for me?" If you perceive that there is nothing in it for you, be transparent and clear and ask questions again until you find what your gain is. "What does having this goal allow me to do? What does it allow me to experience? What does it stop from happening?" Be clear, be open, and be transparent.

Be sure you extract your gain with enough clarity to assess if the value is sufficient. Sometimes we can be heading towards something only to discover the cost to our resources is too high.

Want as much as you need to, and be honest with yourself when creating your goal. In fact the more you search and discover what the benefits for you are, the more certainty you will give your mind.

Intention, expectation, and belief play a significant part in fulfilling a goal. Intention is about purpose, expectation is about anticipation, and belief is the ability to perceive the outcome as attainable for you.

Make certain of your intention. It is important that your intention is in keeping with your goal. Your intention contains and therefore reveals your values and your integrity. It's the reason behind your reason for doing something.

If you are acting for the benefit of satisfying another person and their needs, you may find that your motivation is diminished and your level of satisfaction limited. Or, you may need to acknowledge that your goal is to feel good when satisfying others.

Chapter 17

Values are the benefits received from our experiences. There are different types of values we can strive for. It is important to grasp that the benefits to one person may be different than the benefits to another.

For example, two people may want a steady relationship. One seeks the benefits of having someone to spend time travelling and sharing experiences whilst the other seeks the comfort of having someone at home where they can be taken care of.

Neither of the above is wrong, they are just different. To each the value is the benefit they will have from their goal and may not be of much value to someone who enjoys their autonomy.

There are several areas to consider when setting out to implement a change in direction. Clearly identify which values you are seeking and examine how they will benefit you.

On some level and to some degree we all have expectations. It is important to address some of the issues that arise from expectation. It may seem like common sense to assume that if we set goals we need on some level to be expecting to achieve them.

Notice if in the past you have mostly felt accomplished or disappointed with the outcome of your goals.

If you have set goals and expected them and mostly accomplished them, then it is wise to continue doing what you are doing and keep getting the results.

If on the other hand you have frequently found yourself disappointed then I would suggest that you review your expectations. They may be unrealistic. The change of direction you seek may be ill defined. In the questionnaire section of this book the final question will help minimize the possibility of this happening.

Perhaps here there is a pattern for disappointment, believing that your expectations are reasonable and that the world is somehow conspiring against you.

One thing is for sure, if you keep doing and thinking what you have always done and thought, you are likely to keep experiencing what you have always experienced.

This can sometimes be caused by arrogance or the need to perpetuate victimization where a mindset is so fixed in its rightness that it can allow no room for possibilities that lie outside of its perception. Fixed views stop perception from identifying anything, other than what has been pre-decided.

Consider a person who decides that the new position he has been moved to at work is not going to work for him. He has decided he will not like the new position before he has taken time to think it through.

Sometimes the reason for this is that we have adapted and now habitually only see the negative in a situation; perhaps we simply do not have the skills to think about events and limit our perspective to first impressions.

Being blindsided certainly diminishes perceptual agility and restricts some of us to wander around in our circles of rightness. What can help is to step mentally into a place that allows perception to expand and review the broader picture. To do this simply requires that we gather information without judgment.

Imagine meeting yourself somewhere and having a conversation about your mindset and attitude. What advice would you receive? Would you hear that you need to adapt to a mindset that is more determined or that you need to be less rigid?

This exercise may sound easy to do yet I have found many struggling to explore this kind of self-examination. Have a go as best you can and explore the possibilities.

There is another perspective to consider. You will need to examine your own belief about your worthiness. You may be held back by a belief that you can't have more out of life.

This is a view that you will need to review and renegotiate. It is probably linked to some past guilt or may have been simply programmed in childhood. Explore and challenge if that is the case.

It is important to develop expectations that are in keeping with the kind of mindset that best suits your future needs. By that, I mean that if disappointment causes you distress then simply set your goal and be detached and indifferent to the outcome. Only allow yourself to enjoy the full extent of your accomplishment when you have it.

This may sound like a contradiction, and in some ways it is, yet for many it is a way to avoid being disappointed. It requests a "we will see how things pan out" mindset while progress is being made.

This attitude helps to minimize the creation of negative emotions. It could be that you develop a philosophy that accepts that sometimes things turn out differently. It is useful to make the best of however things turn out.

A healthy expectation is one where you are proceeding with correct persistence and an attitude that feels right for the outcome, no matter what that is.

It could also be that it is not so much that the goal is unrealistic, rather that you have not evaluated your resources accurately. If you think you can accomplish more than your resources can deliver, you are likely to be left wanting.

A worthwhile exercise is to evaluate your resources and ensure that you utilize every available avenue when the time comes. Having said this, do not underestimate your own mind's abilities to manifest goals that appear a little way off.

Resources build upon resources. You may have evaluated your resources in the past and not realized that each passing day you have developed new skills and strengthened your existing skills.

This enables you to do more today than you could perhaps have done yesterday. Our mental abilities expand in a different time frame than our physical abilities. The latter seem to peak in our prime and slow down with the passing of time.

Chapter 18

Notice how sometimes things happen in the most unexpected ways. You might have wondered how you would ever find someone to get into a relationship with. With no possibilities in sight you might have felt that it would be impossible. The next thing you know you're out with a friend when you bump into a friend of theirs.

Suddenly you find yourself spending most of the evening chatting, and at the end of the evening exchanging telephone numbers. The next thing you know you are in a relationship. How could you have planned this?

Some might say that it was just luck. I suggest that it is an open mind seeking an opportunity, recognizing it and grabbing it. Things turn out best for those of us who choose to accept opportunities that enhance the quality of our lives.

It is sometimes wondrous how things turn out for people who operate with an open mind. Such people are focused on the goals and are prepared when things need to be dealt with. When looking backwards at how things turned out, you might think that miracles were happening. That is your mind at work.

Your mind is, when focused on a goal, more than capable of accomplishing it if it is left to its own devices. It seeks opportunities, and if none exists it will create opportunities. It seeks to fulfill your needs and wants. It just requires you to stay clear minded, focused, determined and uncompromising in your quest.

The exact way the mind works is still to a large degree unknown. There has been progress made by the likes of Edward de Bono and Steven Pinker, yet we are still left perplexed to a large degree.

To know we exist, we need to be experiencing something. And if the mind can create an environment where it can experience with a degree of certainty, all is well.

Much frustration can arise when our passion is suppressed and unable to find a vent for expression. It may even be a forbidden desire.

The challenge is finding a balance between stability, experience and expression.

Change is a challenge in the sense that it destabilizes the system and creates a feeling of apprehension at one end of the scale to dread at the other. The degree to which we can cope with this is dependent on past experiences. Let's be clear that not all change is good change. Sometimes mistakes are made and consequences need to be considered.

We can spend hours seeking to fully understand the mechanics of the mind or we could simply utilize what we do know. Just as we use electricity produced at a power plant, we do not need to understand the principle of nuclear fusion to know how to use an electric kettle. It is enough to know that there are limitations to what it can do and what we can know.

Chapter 19

Not infrequently you may find it difficult setting goals on the basis that you have too many options. This can be the mind being bullied by opportunities. There is so much choice that we cannot commit to anything. A thinking tool that allows a quality evaluation would be useful to learn if this is happening to you.

Having too much choice can be debilitating and frustrating. When opportunities are missed this can further fuel our frustration. It can become a repeating pattern where no action is taken because the choices are too many. The ease of doing something is the trap. It all becomes very convenient.

Sometimes it is perceived as procrastination when in fact we do not know what the best option is. Blinded by the richness of choice we wait for clarity. Often by the time we get there, the opportunity has passed. Often it is the delay that causes its demise.

There is also the possibility that having choice is the end goal. In other words the goal is not to feel trapped. You may have the view that you can feel free in your situation so long as you believe that you can escape it any time. So long as you have options you are OK.

Choice can be "a trap" by another name. It can be just another way of staying stuck in the current situation. Explore whether or not evidence exists to validate this by performing a historical review. Just notice if that has been a factor on your frustration levels.

A solution is to review the big picture. What would you like to experience in your life? A question such as "What is imperative and must happen in my lifetime?" might help. What needs to happen by the time we reach our day of reckoning? Make a point of validating and even setting into action a parallel goal to set that in motion.

It could be that we become so uncertain of our own thinking that we are no longer sure about our own decisions. We may spend hours asking others what they think about something before we act. The probability is that we are left as perplexed as we started.

Uncertainty can be further perpetuated by those who respond by asking a question and then reply to the answer with a question. For example a woman might ask her friend, "Do you think I look all right?" The friend responds, "Yes, you look great"; then the questioner asks, "Do you think so?"

The doubts build up like lime scale and eventually amounts to an inability to accept anything that is thought or said. Doubts tend to be expressed in statements such as: Is it? Does it? Was it? Can it? Do you think so? Really? This type of doubt does nothing to develop certainty. As a point of interest, it can also become tiring to the people who have to constantly reassure the doubter.

A value matrix helps to minimize the choices and can help to show the most likely best choice. Write down all your options then complete the matrix. Select the choice that requires the least amount of energy and provides the maximum pleasure or best experience. Having decided, use that as your goal and complete the goal setting program (a sample value matrix is printed in the back of this book and is available online).

Another major consideration in getting more out of life is the resources available to you. Often it appears that people aspire for a lot more than their resources can deliver. There is a sort of "I deserve more" or "I should have more" perspective.

If you feel this way you may need to review your concept of life and what you are or are not entitled to based on what evidence. Challenge limiting beliefs at every junction. The "says who" attitude can help here.

On the other hand it could be that the resources you believe you have are overvalued. You might have been set up for failure by being overly praised during a childhood developmental period.

In this case a child is told endlessly, "You are the best, you will be a great star, you are going to be a fantastic surgeon, you will be the best footballer and you're going to be better than everyone." You may have your own statement to add to the list.

These types of comments are as damaging as the negative ones that some people reading this book will have experienced. The pressure that this puts on a child is colossal. Sooner or later he or she discovers that there is someone who can do something better. For some, it's just too much. They stop and settle down into normality often referred to as "average."

This requires a moment of objective clarity. Perhaps seek another person's opinion to re-evaluate your circumstances and skills. This may also be picked up by the person validating your goals. Just as we may need a mechanic, a financial advisor or a doctor to give us an assessment, we may need a coach or mentor to assess our capabilities.

In some instances you may well undervalue your resources and be unable to see that you are more than capable of fulfilling your needs. This is not uncommon and can tend to originate from being undervalued or insufficiently encouraged in the past.

The solutions are to evidence to yourself by writing down without judgment all capabilities from being able to drive or use an underground map to speaking other languages. Everything that you can be aware of being able to do helps to validate and empower your mind into action. Generating a new skill is always an option and may be the subject of another book.

You may not feel that what you do is in any way special, and may even be embarrassed at writing it all down. You might find it helpful to just write your talents down as a list of characteristics, ignoring the importance or unimportance. They are simply facts about you.

Or it could be that you do not perceive what you are doing as important or relevant. You might struggle to find anything you do as being worth mentioning. This simply requires that you consider that for everything you do, there is a very high chance that there is someone out there who can't.

Simply recognize that even having sight is ability. By compiling a very detailed list and exploring the characteristics, you might discover you are more resourced than you think (check out the Website for some inspiration).

Chapter 20

It is good to keep abreast of your current resources and assets.

Your state of:

Health - Your health is critical in that it strengthens or limits your overall ability to function.

Energy - Your energy is like a rechargeable battery. There is a limit to what can be achieved day by day. Invest your energy wisely.

Time - Your time is perhaps the most precious of your resources. It is very limited and irreplaceable.

Skills -Through life there are many things we learn such as communicating, driving, negotiating a loan, speaking another language, computer literacy, teaching, etc. These are some of your skills.

Wealth - Money accumulated and invested adds to what you can do.

Potential - The ability to expand your resources is a potential. It is what you are capable of doing that you have not yet done.

Imagination/Perceptual agility - The ability to view situations from varying angles gives both greater breadth and depth, further increasing understanding.

Common sense - Those who have a healthy degree of common sense tend to undervalue its worth. Something that might be obvious to you can perplex another. This ability is so undervalued. Life can be very difficult for people who do not have much of it.

Network -The people you associate with all add value to your life. Huge industries depend on connectivity to people. Someone with a good network can benefit from other people's knowledge and associations. The wider the network, the more possibilities arise.

Chapter 21

Perceived obstacles can put you off setting goals. When a solution cannot be found in advance, you might quit without taking time to explore options. A key point to bear in mind is that not all solutions exist in advance of the goals completion.

Sometimes we might not know how to overcome an obstacle. It is often possible that the solution will appear en route. It may even be that the solution is only found when wrestling with the challenge.

You may have an idea to start a business in Web design. It could be that the marketing of the product may not be known at the design stage.

Yet if you strive toward the goal, you might discover that the office next door, a recruitment company, needs your services. In return they will do a swap and place your literature in their mail-out to introduce you to some of their clients. This could not have been evident at the offset.

Generally the non-starters are those who want absolute certainty before they set their goal. There are many still waiting whilst others are getting on. People are not born experts; they become experts by applying what they learn on their journey.

A degree of uncertainty may just be a fact of life and perhaps needs to be accepted if you are struggling. A logical stance to adopt is to discover what degree of certainty you need and accept that for you this is comfortable.

Accepting that the scales of success will tip with the more certainty you have, though it may never be able to totally tilt the scales, may help keep your mind clear and focused.

Put-downs are occasionally used by those who find it difficult to see others progress and improve their lot in life. They can range from a throwaway remark such as "yeah right, and you think you can get through university" to "who on earth is going to take someone like you on?" These types of remarks are designed to destroy any aspirations in an instant.

Some people will use sabotage to ensure that we make no progress. This can leave us confused, especially if the destruction is being created by someone who we believe to be on our side. Look to monitor and understand what the dynamics are within all your relationships. Saboteurs tend to be within our social network. They are people who we know.

Meddlers are another form of hindrance. Mostly it tends to be people who want to be helpful and lack sufficient common sense or understanding. They are simply interfering with the process and getting you in a muddle. It may be that they are involving themselves in situations that damage the progress being made.

Cynicism is another source of damage. Cynics tend to have a wonderful way of showing contempt for your opportunities. They shine a torch on the dark side of the goal with such gusto and enthusiasm. It is, after all, much easier to criticize than to praise. The reward for criticism is instant.

Distance is the solution. Get as far away as possible from those types of conversation. The error is to assume that you can educate these people. That is not their intention. They know the game they have designed better than you and they will always win.

Needy and dependent individuals can absorb a great deal of your energy. They tend to be people who want to help so long as they are needed. They can also ensure that their help to you is just short of what you may need to accomplish your goal if the goal ultimately means them not being needed any longer.

Dreamers and hyperrealists can also interfere with the goal at hand. Some can take a goal and distort it to an unrecognizable mess. A person seeking a printing shop on the high street tells a friend of their plan. The conversation led by the friend suddenly becomes a conversation about creating a national magazine. Keep focused on the goal that has been understood and set by you and avoid engaging with dreamers who are likely to blur your vision.

Well-intentioned people who want to help can sometimes be a hindrance. The degree of fear they have experienced in their life can affect the way they approach future ventures. Their tendency is to be overly cautious, and they can display unrealistic degrees of worry. If you take their counsel, extract what is useful and leave the rest.

When we change direction in life and are seeking to make improvements for ourselves, the assumption that everyone in our life wants us to make progress is incorrect. At times it may be prudent to keep some of our plans confidential until they have materialized.

Remember that you are a part of everyone else's change possibility, and consequently you may experience a degree of resistance from some people.

"Delay always breeds danger; and to protract a great design is often to ruin it."

Miguel de Cervantes

Chapter 22

Obligation and duty can play a significant part in the change process. This occurs when our needs and wants are in conflict with our obligations.

There may be situations that arise where your action conflicts with a strong sense of duty. It could be that you have parents, partners, or children whose needs and wants are dependent upon you.

These are commitments that need to be considered. If you have committed to a partner and your intention is to spend your life together, then it is reasonable to expect that you will need and want to fulfill your obligations to the union. Any changes you seek to implement need to consider your partner, children, etc.

Clarify the degree of your dutifulness and obligations. Are they implied or spoken openly? Have you, by default, taken on a responsibility that you actually do not need to take on or perhaps one that has been hoisted on you? Is the situation that you find yourself in one you have agreed with your partner?

If things change to the degree that you can no longer identify yourself with them, then perhaps there is a strong need to action change.

It's a little like going to help someone in his shop and after a few weeks finding yourself unable to detach from that situation. It may be that you have created a situation that you find hard to disengage from.

Being stuck in this way can create a feeling of resentment. Be aware of what needs to happen to make appropriate changes. There is likely to be a degree of discomfort when making such a shift. Better a degree of discomfort that a lifetime of discontent.

Self-help books often encourage affirmations and positivity in daily doses. This can be dangerous if you do not know what you are doing. Affirmations need to be truisms. That means you need to say things about yourself and your abilities that are true and more importantly that are meant.

You might not appreciate that damage is being caused by saying something that you do not believe to be a fact about you. Having said this, do not be put off, as you have many positive truths about you that you can acknowledge. You may just have to look a little more closely at yourself.

To affirm something that is meant is an affirmation. Affirmations may work for some people and in some places yet they are no substitute for the action required to bring about a change in direction.

Simply affirm something that is meant. Do not equate size of accomplishment with affirmation or self-praise. There are many things that can be accomplished by habitually validating something positive about you and your mind. You can confirm that you have accomplished many things and therefore a correct affirmation would be "I learn".

Consider everything from passing a driving test or learning something in the past confirms that you can accomplish. And perhaps the most important of accomplishments is the ability to read and absorb information. To learn is something most of us can do.

A point to bear in mind about good goal setting is this: if you have nothing good to say about yourself it's best to say nothing and just get on until you do have something good to say.

Sometimes people settle for less than they are capable of getting. In some ways this is understandable for someone who fears not getting there.

A manager that won't step up for a directorship in case he or she makes a mistake, another that settles for an "average" person in a relationship when he could be with someone outstanding. It's not a question of right or wrong. It is our right to exercise our choice based on the information available to us and our perceived resources.

Willfulness is vital for the process of reaching your goal. Willfulness is correct persistence as opposed to anger. What is not prudent is to be driven towards your goal by resentment or hatred. The chemical effect this has on our organism is severely damaging and may result in causing irreparable damage.

There is an option for those who are starting from a disadvantaged beginning and have little self-certainty. People who were never told they could aspire to more need to apply themselves a little more only until it becomes easier.

Accountability for this outcome requires you to consider the players involved in accomplishing this outcome. The focus here is to give clarity to the mind as to the people involved for this outcome.

The fewer people involved in the outcome, the greater the chance of accomplishment. Systems with fewer components stand a lesser chance of a breakdown. Simplicity rules here.

Excuses could include "They won't help me with my CV so how can I get a job?" or "I can't drive so how am I supposed to socialize and make friends?" or "These forms are so complicated and there is so much to do, I can't get into a university to study."

It is game over if you excuse yourself for not accomplishing. I might suggest that you turn it on its head and use excuses for doing rather than not doing. Sympathize with your strength rather than your weakness.

Accepting accountability and responsibility for your life's outcomes is important if you are to strengthen your mind's resolve to act. You are responsible for the goal you set and for the journey you choose to make.

Acknowledge that some things may happen by chance, coincidence and serendipity, but mostly they happen by design. Accept that you are responsible for the change in direction.

Occasionally you may experience a degree of self-doubt, an uncertainty that any progress is being made. There are times when the captain of a ship alters the direction to head to new coordinates.

He knows that from the time he was given the new coordinates to the time they have been implemented there will be lapses of time where for several miles it will appear the ship is not heading in the new direction.

Being accountable and taking the responsibility for your outcomes is perhaps one of the most empowering actions you can take. All too often we play the blame game as a way of avoiding taking responsibility for our lives.

> "Take your life in your own hands, and what happens? A terrible thing: no one to blame."
>
> Erica Jong

To have a greater degree of control in your life, being in the driving seat and choosing where you go requires that you take responsibility for the decisions you do and do not make and act upon.

For some seeking change, it may be best to be as detached as possible from the process and the outcome until you have got there. Then connect to your accomplishment and appreciate it by reveling in it whilst pondering on your next goal.

Chapter 23

Occasionally glitches occur, just as sometimes you can step on something unpleasant in the street. You have a choice in what you do next.

- You can sit there in disbelief at how this could possibly have happened to you of all people. How could this be?

- You can feel embarrassed and hide it hoping that no one notices, and scuttle away feeling ashamed.

- You can spend time looking to find the person responsible and tell yourself through gritted teeth that you will give them a mouthful when you catch up with them.

- You can sit and inspect it on your shoe, deeply exploring exactly what this is and what it means. Perhaps it's a hidden message or something.

- You can arrange never to walk down the street again and go the long way round.

- You can take your tale and tell all your friends how bad the situation in the street is getting.

- You can write to your local government complaining about the conditions on the street and even start a blog about it.

- Or you can wipe your shoe and get on to where you're going.

Awareness of the environment you are in and a quick assessment of this happening again could be useful. If it appears that this has happened more often than not it may be useful to avoid that side of the street or simply take precautions.

Chapter 24

Timing is everything, yet all too often we tend to ignore this fact. It is critical to set a time frame for a goal to be reached. An unspecified goal to be reached at an unspecified time results in an unspecified outcome at an unspecified time.

The section on time in the goal setting section requires diligence in its setting. This is something that can understandably be perplexing for some people. Things can happen in minutes, hours, days or years.

The solution is to explore some events from the past and examine how fast things happened and how frequently the unexpected occurred.

For example, say you want to play football and have nowhere to go. You mention this to the barman who points to someone at the bar and tells you that he organizes a local team. The next thing you know you are practicing. The whole thing happened in hours. You might say that it was just coincidence. Call it what you will, it still happened.

Coincidence is a wondrous happening that can be often confused with chance or luck. Consider luck as being an open mind seizing an opportunity. Chance, on the other hand, is the coming together of random acts to create an identifiable event.

Coincidence occurs when your "needs and wants" are in harmony. In other words, when there is no conflict your attention is more focused. The following diagram depicts the process.

When needs and wants come together, coincidence occurs.

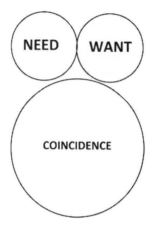

Things just appear to happen. Opportunities suddenly become more frequent and more apparent. It is up to you to recognize it as an opportunity. Just start to accept coincidence as a part of your change process.

There are many options available to us. We can head in any direction, opt for a number of vocations, partner with any number of people, develop ideas in a number of areas, and adopt a number of different attitudes. The choices are virtually limitless and the talent is in the choices.

The ability to think in a particular way and choose a particular direction is about as close to freedom of choice as we are likely to get. It is worthwhile setting aside time to explore the various mindsets available and choose the one that best fits your needs and wants. There is a fine balance to keep between stability, excitation and resources.

Changing direction is not discouraged; it only requires a degree of caution. If you find yourself constantly changing direction on matters that are significant, you may need to first overcome the trap of indecision. Explore and discover if you are able to appreciate what life has to offer.

You might discover that your journey to becoming an accountant highlights your ability to research and present your findings. This leads you to doing something in the media. Possibilities often arise on the journey to your goal.

The journey often offers many opportunities, a little like road junctions that you come across when going someplace. You may choose to change direction. It is your prerogative, and ultimately you are accountable for where you take yourself in life. Change simply facilitates your desires.

Indecision is infrequent in our everyday life. Mostly we know what we want and what to avoid. Frequently a decision not to decide can be confused with indecision.

Best acknowledge it as such and decide that a decision has been taken not to decide. You may find this more empowering than wandering around undecided. Make the decision to decide to stay undecided. You may find it beneficial to set a time in the future when you will make a decision.

Chapter 25

A change of direction or goal requires a kick-start if it is ever to manifest. Just as an aircraft needs to reach a pre-required speed to be able to take off the ground, so, too, you will need to ensure that sufficient impetus has been given to activate and commit your mind towards a goal.

The most progressive step that can be taken towards your goal is critical and a vital factor in the process. If you need to find new employment and say that the most progressive step is to get the trade papers and see who is advertising, you are suggesting that buying the paper is the most you are prepared to do. Perhaps applying for a job might take you closer.

The chances of getting into new employment by buying a trade paper are close to zero. This goal is unlikely to get off the ground.

Similarly, if you are seeking a relationship and suggesting that the most progressive step you can take is to get your hair done, you are highly unlikely to reach your goal - unless someone comes calling perhaps.

Taking the most progressive step requires thought and courage. It is the step that encourages and commits the mind to the goal. To be courageous is risky; not to could be worse.

When all is said and done a desired outcome remains a desire if there is no action or where the action fails to create the necessary momentum to propel you toward your goal.

The types of goal that can be set are endless. It is probably useful to loosely categorize them as short medium and long term goals.

Short - imminent goals that need to happen within the year.

Medium - goals set over a one to three year period.

Long - goals set over a three to five year period.

I added another category for myself which I call my Life Goals. This, I think, is self-explanatory and has given me plenty to look forward to in the future and much to appreciate from past accomplishments. Having a list of must-do things before you reach your terminus helps prepare the mind to achieve those things.

Goals can be set in parallel so that you can be heading to several new experiences at the same time. Simply ensure that there is congruence. That is to say that there is a common thread with the goals set. Setting a goal to be in a relationship is unlikely to happen if you want to go out with your group of friends every night.

Having a goal that sets out to be in a local darts team may well not be in keeping with another goal of wanting to work as a croupier. Your hours of work will conflict with your other interest. A degree of common sense needs to be applied.

Future goal setting is part of the *Change Directions* goal-setting process. Setting a goal that follows the current goal adds another little something to the minds need for stability.

Knowing that there is a continuation and a glimpse as to what it will be adds to the minds need for certainty.

Stability is maintained, and the knowledge that there is a continuation to your life after this goal has been reached further adds certainty to the mind.

Planning ahead also creates an opportunity for the mind to prepare for the next goal. The process runs in the background just as a computer can be performing duties while we continue to use it; so, too, the mind prepares for the next event.

Occasionally the desired change is not achieved. This can be caused by unspecified or unforeseeable events. The fact is that your goal did not happen. It may be useful to review your position and check that there are no causes within your activities or beliefs.

It may well be that your starting point is too far from your target or that the goal is too ambitious. It could also be that your target lacks motivation and the reward lacks potency. Review and move on.

Your destination might be one of those places that the mind has difficulty in understanding and is stuck. Review the goal by spending some time exploring and extracting a clearer meaning and purpose. This might highlight some errors.

Another wonderful thing about the mind is that it has an ability to create a virtual reality. The tools we have as human beings are many and varied. One of these outstanding abilities is to simulate an experience in our mind in a kind of virtual world. This arena is commonly called our imagination.

Our imagination allows us to create hypothetical situations and experience them in the safety of our minds. Visioning may seem unexciting to some yet it is an ability that can save us a great deal of heartache and allows us to explore possibilities in the future and test the outcome before we get there.

Some people may need to explore visioning with a greater degree of caution if they have a propensity for the catastrophic. If you tend to easily see the dark side of a situation you may need to increase the time spent exploring the benefits. I might even suggest that you seek some professional assistance.

Consider the imagination as a training area, a place where you are rehearsing the goal and the steps which lead to its accomplishment.

This element prepares us for the journey to come by minimizing the fear of the unknown. It therefore helps to create a degree of certainty in the mind.

Chapter 26

You may find it helps to have a fallback position. This assists to ease anxiety or fear in the event that the primary goal is not achieved.

This can be a double-edged sword though. You could be aiming for a managerial position and be prepared to accept a supervisory role. It is possible that a habit forms and the mind repeatedly accepts the easy option.

Where a pattern of fallback positions becomes the norm, it may be prudent to explore the possibility of creating a deliberate mental stretch by aiming higher and deciding not to settle for second best.

There are times when we need to look beyond the facts. Facts are essential and vital to the outcome. We do have another ability that, in my opinion, has been neglected and allowed to some degree to perish. Our ability to *sense* allows us to simply feel a situation without justification like an emotional snapshot of the current focus.

Those of you who have embraced the *Six Hats* thinking will understand the importance of the red hat. For those who have not, I have included a very brief explanation.

We are feeling creatures and have emotional reactions to situations that we cannot always put into words. Often we tend not to express these feelings because of our belief that we need to justify our feelings with some kind of reasoned evidence. It is prudent to express feelings, whether positive or negative, and treat these as valid forms of information, in conjunction with our goals.

By incorporating our senses into our goal, we are utilizing the combined neural network as a resource to give an overall reading of our mind's emotional interpretation of a situation without justification. It then is treated as another piece of valid information and has its place in the design of the goal.

The questions that follow this section are designed to allow your mind to focus intensely on your goal. There is no room for selflessness here - not that I have ever encountered it. If such a thing exists I have not found it.

The goals you set need to be about you and for you if you are to minimize failure and maximize success.

Setting a goal to make someone else happy or wanting someone else to be more giving may not be the wisest thing to do. Accepting responsibility for your self is hard enough without taking on the responsibility for others who may not want it anyway.

Some people are happy enough experiencing drama. It could be that without drama and tragedy their life lacks meaning and could even become boring for them. It tends to be people with a hysterical disposition that are most prone to create dramas.

They are able to create a drama out of just about anything. It creates an experience of existence for them. Without this dramatization of life's events, what would exist?

How relevant and appropriate is your reaction to what is going on for other people around you? Separate yourself from drama and theatrics and people who exhibit these hysterical traits.

Accept that some people with characteristics of victimization are not seeking to be rescued. On most occasions I have found that there is little I can offer a martyr that could possibly replace the benefits that their suffering provides.

In any event your mind deals solely with the affairs of your mind and has little or no ability to set goals for others. Only where other people have the will to change will they find the way to redirect their life's experiences.

You creating change may well be the best way to inspire another person to change. The evidence of your change could well be all he or she needs to perceive the possibility.

Goodwill can be better delivered through your actions and accomplishments. Inspiration rather than motivation or manipulation tends to have better long-term results.

Teach through your actions not through your words. Your words are useful, but until you action those words they remain just words.

As well as getting you to where you need to get to, you are teaching others what is possible. When you think for yourself you are not squandering energy and delaying your progress.

Attitudes of apathy or fatalism are perhaps the real killers in the drive towards being the best you can. There is no cure for such a person, who has chosen to give up choice as to how he or she experiences life. Designing future experiences is not on this person's menu of possibilities or desires. These people are best left alone to live life as it happens to them.

People who worry have additional challenges. For them, worry is a real and present experience. It mostly maintains a feeling of fear at what could happen in the future, now. Worry suggests that they are not able to affect future outcomes. It is a very limiting belief.

People who worry have an underling belief that suggests they cannot affect the future. No amount of consoling them seems to last and can seriously deplete resources.

The danger for them is not that they won't stop worrying; it is how much of their resources they could use up seeking to allay their fears. Exercise a degree of caution if such people are part of your plan. They know to worry. They are masters at it. Accept that is what they do best.

If it is you who is accustomed to worrying then it would be prudent to stop and review how worrying has ever helped you in the past. Then consider how it damaged you in the past. No contest.

It may be useful to clarify what I mean when I use the phrase *accept a situation*. By accepting a situation I am not suggesting that you agree with it. I am suggesting that *you* acknowledge it as being what *you* say it is. For example your line manager may speak harshly to you whilst being kind to others. Without criticism accept that as being the case because you cannot change anything unless you have accepted it.

Focus on what is important to you. Focus on the things that really matter. Initially the challenges will revolve around where to start. For most people it is probably related to health, accomplishments, family, happiness, relationships and wealth.

A useful exercise is to create a mind tree. Simply draw a tree and name each branch with an element of your life. Get the big picture first then explore each branch. Decide which branch would benefit you then ponder on the possibilities.

Alternatively, it may help to list your own areas of change. Avoid desperation, as it consumes vast amounts of energy and is, on a deeper level, signaling fear to the mind and causing disbelief that the change is possible.

It is useful to approach change with a degree of curiosity and a desire to explore and experiment. It may also help to take some time and get to know your needs and wants better. Additionally, treat yourself with a high degree of respect and compassion.

I know you may have experienced difficulties in childhood that have resulted in emotional and psychological disorders. Accept this now, understand the affects and move on to your goal.

The result of such damage can leave deep and painful scarring. Do consider that choosing to do things differently is your prerogative and remains entirely in your hands. You can choose a new direction and set your sails. Should you feel yourself unable to get past this it may be useful to seek professional assistance.

In order to set sail in a new direction remember that the anchor needs to be raised, and accept that for a while you may lose sight of land. Letting go of what is, after all, just historic baggage can appear to be difficult at first.

I believe and would encourage you to consider that we have many resources that have not been actively utilized. Over time much programming has been deployed to confuse us and create the illusion of dependence on others. That could include governments, religions, societies, the media, peers, etc. Decide that you have the resources necessary and move to change in ways that add value to your life's experience.

We can all choose to change direction.

We can all seek for what fills us with meaningful experiences. Once again the talent is in the choices. Every action taken results in other possibilities being left. Setting a new direction can mean that other directions may no longer be available thereafter.

Accept that it is not possible to have all that life has to offer. Just as with a meal, you decide to have fish. On this occasion you will forgo all other meats. You might choose a saloon car so you have rejected for the next few years the possibility of an estate or two-door car. In setting a new direction you will have to consider all options then settle for the one that serves your greater good.

Before you set your direction for change, take a moment and spend some time with your list of desired changes, the things you would like to have happen in your life.

Scan for a few more options even though you may be clear; it is worthwhile exploring what else is available. Do a 360° view and explore what else is possible. You might discover that more is possible and decide that you want more. Some areas are suggested in the back of this book.

Time is a serious matter that needs to be covered. Time is required to complete the process. There is one sure way of ensuring that little changes; keep talking about doing whilst never actually committing yourself to paper. Now is a good time to start committing. Why else would you have bought this book?

As mentioned previously, if you keep doing what you have always done there is a high probability that you will keep getting what you have always got.

"Problems cannot be solved by the same level of awareness that created them."

Albert Einstein

Decide the direction that you wish to take, and as best you can explore the benefits that they could lead you to. Then use your resources to get to them.

One thing is for sure, the type, quality and style of thinking that has got you this far in life will need to change if you are to create new experiences in your life.

Some beliefs about life and your relationship to life will need to be transformed. Walking your talk is the fastest way to begin. Yourself-talk needs to be calm and certain. Be gentle with yourself when you need to be. At times you may just need to be very willful.

Your mindset needs to reflect the kind of mindset that helps and doesn't hinder the process for change.

Chapter 27

The ability to perceive your desired outcome is critical. Many books are available on getting to your dreams. They often talk about visualization as a means of setting a goal. I have some concerns about this.

Only a portion of the population has the ability to create full-color images in their minds. The rest could believe that not "seeing" it means it is not available. This is not so.

Without detracting from the matter at hand, I would suggest that perception is not just about what you "see". It is more about what you sense. This includes all your senses (sight, sound, touch, smell and taste).

For some people it is the taste of success that motivates them, whist for others it is the image. Find the medium that your mind favors and use it.

Neuro-linguistic programming (NLP) deals with some elements of perception differently. Our internal representation of what we experience can differ from one person to another. Although most of us can see, hear and feel, the degree to which we can do these things is not necessarily the same for all.

Some might see very well while others have outstanding hearing. Some are able to feel at a depth that others cannot reach. This is just our way of representing what is going on in our mind.

Perception is a matter of choice to a great degree, though our tendency is to perceive something one way, and that becomes the default.

This can be avoided by reviewing certain attitudes and opinions you have. Deliberately set out to explore how many other ways something could be perceived; then select the one that best serves you.

You can choose to see the glass half empty whilst someone else hasn't even noticed the glass and is focused on the spilt water. A third person may see an opportunity to sell napkins; it's all a matter of choice. Understand how your mind operates by default, and ensure that it is in keeping with your desired changes.

Chapter 28

The second part of this book is about the process for changing directions. The questions are designed to give you an opportunity to engage with your mind at a level that perhaps you have not experienced in the past.

The process can take a while and I would suggest that you make and set the time so that you can be focused, refreshed and, most of all, ready for change. A sober attitude with determination adds to the gravitas of your intention.

There are probably many areas that you would like to bring change to and the temptation may be to deal with the ones that cause you the most discomfort. It may be prudent to explore all areas first, as there may be a priority of sequence to follow.

Thinking about the long-term objective initially may also be useful. Check to see that you do not have overly conflicting meta systems.

That is to say that you are not caught up in two or more systems that do not cohabitate easily. Where you experience internal conflict, the likelihood is that you will encounter frustration.

An example of this may be if you are religiously inclined and running a business; there may be a conflict with what the business requires of you and what your faith teaches. You may need to clarify how this will work for you and accept that it is your choice ultimately.

Decide how you want to deal with this by choosing your priorities carefully. You need to decide and accept that others may not have chosen the same, as they have different priorities. You will know the right choice for you by the degree of joy or relief you experience with your decision.

There are probably times when you will need to push yourself to get to an answer. It can help to use a specific time period to answer a question. Say you set a time of around five minutes maximum for a question. You may be surprised how when the mind is left to decide on an action without being bound to time it takes more than is necessary. The solution is to give your mind a time to reach a conclusion to the question.

It may take longer the first time you engage in the process than future goals you might set. The more practiced you are the easier it gets. I would suggest that you avoid falling into the trap of thinking that if you just think your goal it will be enough.

The ability to be able to design in thoughts seems to work well with children whose minds are mostly untainted with what they can't do. So avoid the mind's ability to avoid change and commit your design to paper.

I might suggest that you read through the rest of the book before setting off to complete it. Get a flavor for what you will be engaging in.

It may be practical to use a pencil in the questions section as it will allow you to go back and revisit the questions and make any adjustments that you sense appropriate.

I have used the word *goal* to describe the desired outcome, and occasionally these phrases are interchanged. In any event, *goal* in context of this book includes elements of your intention, your purpose, your aim and your objective.

Although these terms have differing meanings, for the purpose of this book I use the word *goal* as the place you need and want to reach.

The next section is all about helping you direct a goal and implement change in one or more areas of your life. In reading this far, you have already expanded your understanding on the subject of change, and that will have you thinking slightly differently about how you approach the desire for change.

This book is about designing change and is, as mentioned previously, the point at which some will withdraw from engaging in the process. If you decide that this is not something that you wish to engage in, simply accept this and move on with your life.

If you decide to engage in the process, begin in earnest and immerse yourself in it. Change is something that inevitably happens. Directing some elements of that change is possible for you to engage in if you want to drive your own mind.

You may have noticed that there is a very appealing aspect when you meet people who know where they are going. There is strength about them. They have a presence that radiates purpose.

"The whole world steps aside for the man who knows where he is going."

Anon

Decide what you would like to have happen in your life, and then design, prepare and implement for change.

The degree of change that you may want to consider engaging in will depend on how comfortable you are in your life. You must answer this question; it cannot be answered on your behalf.

"Nature abhors a vacuum, and if I can only walk with sufficient carelessness I am sure to be filled."

Henry David Thoreau

Consider how comfortable it is being you. How cope-able is your life? The greater the discomfort and the level of demands placed upon you, the greater insight as to how much change you need to consider implementing. Do not be selfless here. Do take a view that will help in creating a better life for you.

Consider also that the way you feel about life may not necessarily be as a consequence of something that is happening. It could be rather that the feeling of unease is caused by insufficient challenges in your life. Simply select something to do for the challenge.

The more pleasurable life is, the less change is required. That does not mean that change is unnecessary, rather that you may choose to create change for the new experiences.

Focusing and directing your mind uses a great deal of energy. Being aware and concentrating for the length of time required may be a little challenging.

There is no need to complete the process in one sitting, though I have found that most people who have done so found it easier. It may take two to four hours.

It may be prudent to allow a day or so to elapse having read through this entire book, and then begin the design process.

It is useful to keep your answers clear and concise. Get the essence down in as few words as possible. Keep it simple and understandable. Avoid unnecessary detail. Stick to defining your goal.

A quick reminder that your mind will probably look to avoid any changes being planned by you. Be vigilant, be determined and most of all, be ready to change directions.

Chapter 29

The Goal-setting Section

"Our goals can only be reached through a vehicle of a plan, in which we must fervently believe, and upon which we must vigorously act. There is no other route to success."

Stephen A. Brennan

Question 1:

What I would like to have happen specifically?

In other words: What do I need and want specifically? What is my goal? What is my idea? What is my desired outcome?

This section is about setting a direction that you require your mind to take. Choose a goal and focus on it. The question that needs answering is very specific and may take a few goes to refine and make concise.

A little time is required for this first question, so I would urge you to make the necessary time available to think through your areas for change.

I will give a brief overview of the elements that you may need to consider when selecting your desired outcome.

Consider all the different areas of your life. Your personal life - how comfortable it is being you? How well are your partnerships and relationships, be they social, professional, vocational, recreational, educational, etc. working for you?

Look at each area as if you are above and seeing yourself experiencing it. Select the area where you are going to create change.

Explore the different options that are available and ponder as to which option will bring about the best reward for you. Avoid jumping on the first idea that comes to you, as perhaps there are better ideas a little further down the line that may prove to be more rewarding.

Make certain that you have considered the various factors involved, and think about what for you is the most important priority that the change must fulfill.

Consider generally the consequences and sequel to the change being made. Think about it generally as you will have an opportunity to fully explore this a little later. Project into the future and get a sense of where this will lead you. Be happy with the outcome.

Where the options are many and choice appears to be in the balance, use the matrix at the back of the book to help identify the most effective and efficient route forward. If it is a 50/50 choice then it does not matter which you choose.

Ultimately, the power of choice is the greatest resource you have available to you.

This question will be asked in various ways to help define your target. Additionally, the direction you give your mind needs to be constructive and stated positively. This means that stating what you do not want is not a direction. It is as though you are at a crossroads and are telling your mind that you do not want to be where you are.

This does not tell your mind where you need and want to be. So the possibility is that your mind will simply find another situation based on what it knows.

"I need to be an accomplished manager" as opposed to "I should be a better manager" or "I don't want to be a bad manager".

"I need to be in a harmonious relationship" as opposed to "I don't want to be alone anymore".

You can have a great idea that could bring a desired change into your life. If, however, you cannot get your mind to understand it, it may well never happen. Be clear and concise when communicating the idea to your mind. Spend a little longer on reasoning your goal.

Reasoned well, your heart's desire can be the most powerful driving force you possess.

Throughout this section we will use the example of a man seeking to overcome his difficulties with relationships. The challenges he faced arose from a lack of social interaction and criticism during childhood development.

The desired change in direction was reached after much deliberating on the best way to accomplish his needs and wants.

Example:

My goal is:

To have better relationships.

You can ask the question using any one from the list beneath:

What I would like to have happen specifically?

What needs to happen for me?

Where do I need to get to?

What do I need and want specifically?

What do I want to change in my life?

Having explored the possibilities, select the one outcome that defines your target.

State your desire positively.

~

My goal is to...

Question 2:

Redefine my desire

This section is about redefining your goal with two positively stated outcomes.

Having made certain of your needs and wants, it helps further to solidify this in your mind by giving two further definitions. It's a little like the Global Satellite Navigational Systems.

Satellite navigation, or sat-nav as it is more commonly known, works by accessing three or more satellites above the Earth and triangulating our location, providing autonomous geo-spatial positioning. It malfunctions when there are only one or two satellites because it cannot, with any accuracy, tell us where we are or where we need to be.

In the same way we seek to give as much clarity to our mind of the destination by giving a more spatial and broader view of our target.

Having a look at location from one perspective leaves a lot to the imagination as to how it looks from other perspectives. This could be risky, a bit like looking at a building from the front tells us little of how the side or back will look.

Remember, the direction needs to be stated positively.

Redefine my desire. Give at least two additional alternative definitions of the place you need to reach.

Example:

1   Be more socially aware, warm and caring towards those I already know and those I meet.

2   To care for all my relationships from romantic partner to business associates, family and friends.

~

My desire redefined is to ...

1...

My desire redefined again is to ...

2...

Question 3:

What is the concept behind my desired goal?

This section deals with the concept that underpins your desire. What will having your goal do for you? What will it give you? What will it enable you to do?

Concepts are the big picture of a situation. The concept behind a bicycle could be that it is an economical way to travel. It could also be that it is a great way to get fit or that in using it we are reducing carbon emissions.

The concept behind being an accomplished manager could be to deliver better results; it could additionally be that the position leads to better chances for promotion or adding to personal and professional prestige.

Extracting the concept behind your desire to change is a great help to the mind, as it adds clarity and a better understanding.

What is the concept behind my desired goal?

Example:

Be connected to people.

~

Notes:

Question 4:

What will happen or what will be different when I have reached my goal?

This section deals with the consequences and the sequel to the goal having been reached.

How will your circumstances change, how will they be different? What will you be experiencing personally that will enable you to say that you have reached your goal?

What will be different, what will have changed? It is important that your mind can recognize the accomplishment once you are there. I have known people who have passed what they wanted and only realized when it was too late. In most cases this is unrealized. The search continues and ends when the time or energy is no longer available.

Making a perceptual shift that allows you to perceive the goal as if you are there benefits you in several ways.

You will have a better understanding of the intended outcome, as you fill in more detail to the goal. This further clarifies to the mind the experience that is expected.

How will your experiences and understanding be after you have reached the goal? Define as best you can and in as much detail as you are capable of. Use words that mean the right thing for you.

It may alter your feelings about your outcome with the new insight. You may calm any fears or misconceptions that you may have about the proposed changes.

Search for the evidence that will exist when your goal has been accomplished. It could be that the student who is learning new skills will have a certificate of some sort; she will be able to do something that she previously could not. It might be that she will perceive herself applying for a new job with her newfound skills.

On a deeper level, this perceptual stretch validates to some degree that your desired outcome or goal is accomplishable. It also confirms to you that it is the direction you want to head towards. The mind needs to perceive and believe that achievement is possible.

What will happen or what will be different when I have reached my goal?

Example:

I am striking up conversations with anyone at any time.

I am in face to face, phone, and email contact with all my loved ones, partner, friends, family, business associates and clients.

I have a thriving business.

I have a full social life, a place to be whenever I want it.

I have a lot more people in my life, a big network.

A lot more people know and talk about me.

~

Notes: Write about this as if you are there.

Question 5:

Who will be affected by the change I seek?

What effect will other people experience once you have created the change you desire?

It is about exploring the consequences of your actions from the perspective of others around you. Let's suppose that you decide to change your professional direction. You choose to leave your job at the office to become a teacher. You may affect several people around you. You might find that the relationship with your children changes, as you will have more time to spend with them in the summer holidays.

You might find that the degree of personal fulfillment makes you a happier and a more contented person and, consequently, you will be more amiable to those around you.

It could be that the seventy-hour week you were heading towards at the office is reduced and you take time to start playing football and spend more time with friends. All these things have an effect on people around you. Be aware that not all around you may benefit from your change.

Consider the implications and focus on the benefits that will be experienced by others as a consequence of your outcome. More time at home may be a blessing for one person's partner and a nightmare for another's.

Having considered the consequences of your actions upon others, explore how it could affect them in the longer term.

Who will be affected by the change I seek?

Example:

My wife and children, friends, family, clients, business associates, people I meet and people who hear about me.

~

Notes:

Question 6:

What will the goal accomplish for me?

What will the outcome accomplish for you? There is little point in doing something that has no value to you. Where there is no benefit there is a lack of motivation. Search and seek out as many of the benefits from the outcome as you can.

What will the benefits do for you? It is important to be clear as to what the benefits are both for you and those around you that will be affected by you accomplishing your outcome.

Spend time perceiving the benefits of the outcome in the broadest sense. Add as much detail as possible. Detail as many of the possibilities as you can. Avoid only picking the obvious and explore the breadth and depth of the benefits.

Keep in mind to consider the benefit that others may experience as a result of your accomplishment. What will that do for you? For example, it could be that you are experiencing pleasure from the pleasure you are creating for others.

How specifically will you benefit from this change?

What will the goal accomplish for me?

Example:

A happier life, more fulfilled and successful. A deeper love and understanding of people and myself. Boosted and successful business. People will want to be around me and get a lot more pleasure from me, and in time, my life will be filled with more pleasure too. I will have many different types of people in my life, to differing degrees, all decided by me.

~

Notes:

Question 7:

When do I want to reach my goal?

Time frames are extremely important where the mind is concerned. Have you ever found yourself saying that you will do something yet putting it off for as long as possible?

When is the outcome due? This requires consideration and, to some degree, may need to be a guesstimate depending on the outcome sought.

Where the outcome is left with an unspecified end time, you are in jeopardy of waiting for a great length of time, or worse, never accomplishing your outcome.

Direct your attention to the plan and focus on the outcome. Perceive the journey without getting stuck with the elements that are unknown. Experience it as a journey and get a sense of when it is likely to be completed.

You might set time in terms of weeks or months, even years. There might be an element of urgency in your needs and wants that you will need to monitor. Retain a realistic flexibility in the timing of your outcome.

Avoid desperation, as it quickly turns into an underlying fear which the mind translates to keep doing what it knows to do. What is stable becomes the order of the day.

You might want to learn some skills and enter into education. This kind of outcome is probably easier to set a time for. There are programs that you can enroll in with a finite time for completion.

Being too rigid with finding and entering into a relationship is perhaps short-sighted. There need to be considerations beyond the chemical attraction; you may need to invest time to get to know several people before you decide who is best matched to your needs and your strengths and vice versa.

There are many considerations to be taken, such as finding the right environment or the time it may take to develop better skills. A high degree of common sense is necessary in selecting an end time. The momentum needs to be maintained for the outcome to be accomplished. This is much to do about giving yourself sufficient time to act towards your goal whilst not enough time for it to lose appeal.

Use extra caution if you suffer from desperation, frustration or disappointment. All things in life require time to mature. Fruition comes when the outcome is reached.

Do push the boundaries of time a little. You might be surprised at how things can happen very fast at times and in the most unexpected ways.

When do I want to reach my goal?

Day

Month

Year

Question 8:

What information and facts do I have about the goal I seek?

What information do I have about reaching my goal? What do I know about getting to my goal? Here we are talking about facts and facts alone. Facts include financial costs, time costs, energy costs and other resources.

We all need different levels of information in order to reach a decision to act. It is dependent on the seriousness of the change we seek and how we personally operate. Find what works for you.

You will need to be as informed as possible about your intended outcome. You might also consider what others have said about the place you need to reach. Do remember, though, to treat other people's information as second-hand and possibly degraded. Without facts that can be evidenced they are just other people's opinions. Stick to cold hard facts.

In some instances there is information that is simple to access. For example, a person seeking a position as a driving instructor would need to know the rules and conditions prior to application.

Another person might seek to find a partner. It is important to note what your needs and wants are. These are facts, some of which may be non-negotiable to you.

If you are looking to find a match for yourself and are an easy-going, relaxed person who enjoys cooking at home, music, country walks and spending time away from the television talking about pleasurable matters, then you might need to know where people with similar wants and needs tend to congregate.

It would not make sense to hang around the pool section of a pub where the majority enjoy drinking and telling stories in between watching the football on the television and going home half-drunk.

It might make better sense to join an amateur theatre group or a local dance class where, at the very least, you will have some fun in the process of bumping into that special person.

What information and facts do I have about the goal I seek?

Example:

*More time spent connecting with people and less time in isolation.
Initially it will take more of my energy to get the ball rolling – in the
long run, and as long as I take care of my rest time, I think the
outcome will actually give me more energy and reward. I will need
to put my social head on, as a discipline, more often. I may need to
keep a careful eye on past negative habits.*

~

Notes:

Question 9:

What information and facts do I need about the goal I seek?

In your search for information and facts about your intended outcome, you may notice gaps in your knowledge. Explore what information you need which would help better fill in details and direction.

Identifying the information that is required is a major part of giving further assistance to yourself in the accomplishment of your goal.

Let's say your outcome is an MBA in business. You will need to know the facts. How long is the course? What are the costs? How does it deal with delays? How many hours a week? Location and travel time? These types of questions are all significant.

Some information is just interesting and may not appear to add much value to your decision. Still, add it to your list of information as "just interesting". It may ultimately serve to tip the balance. It may be just interesting that a course is held at two colleges that are in the same town, yet the fact that one has a classroom size bigger than the other may help you be more receptive to learning.

This section is about finding out what information is missing and will need to be sought out. It requires spending time to explore what you know that you do not know.

This question asks you to consider furnishing your mind with what it needs to know to get to its objective. It may be that you have access to the information through contacts, network, books, the Internet, etc. in which case you know where to get the information.

If on the other hand you are not clear about where to get the information from, then it would be prudent to get your facts clear before proceeding. You might discover that once you have the information you may want to change your goal. Or you could become more determined to reach it.

What information and facts do I need about the goal I seek?

Example:

Where can I go to, to meet new people? What is it about the way I have interacted with others in the past that needs to change?

~

Notes:

Question 10:

From who or where can I get information and facts about the goal I seek?

If you are aware of missing information, it would be prudent to spend time exploring where best to gain access to people, associations, clubs, books, video, tapes, Websites, etc. that could furnish you with the relevant facts.

It may save you hours of wandering around aimlessly, perhaps exhausting yourself and searching in the wrong area. So time spent accessing sources of information is important.

You may find it difficult to ask for information and would rather do the searching yourself. That, too, is acceptable; just keep in mind that it could take a while longer.

Identifying sources of knowledge is a skill in itself. People employ researchers on the basis that they have the ability to ferret out information.

Therefore, investing time to think about where best to start is a useful activity. It may appear to be wasted time, but in the long run, it not only saves time, it can also add perspectives that you may not have considered.

You might decide to become a councilor for your local borough. It may be useful to meet up with another councilor and find out the process and their personal experience of getting elected. You might talk to a local political party and see what they can offer in terms of information and support.

From who or where can I get information and facts about the outcome I seek?

Example:

Very close friends whose opinion about me and my actions that I can trust. Modelling others who I perceive as being good with respect to my goal. Observing and learning from their behaviour and adapting it to my personality.

~

Notes:

Question 11:

How do I feel about my direction, goal and desired outcome?

This section deals with matters of the heart. It deals with emotions and feelings about the outcome we seek. How do you feel about the outcome you seek?

Let's distinguish between the journey and the arrival. The outcome is more about how you feel about the specific accomplishment. Being there will create in you a feeling of one kind or another.

It is important, at this point, to make clear that we seek feelings about the outcome without justification. You need not explain nor justify why you have these feelings about your outcome. They are simply feelings you have.

The tendency is to explain why we feel what we feel. In this section, justification is discouraged as it can create a negative effect on the outcome.

There seems to be a tendency to express our feelings only when we have the words to justify them. When we have no way of explaining why we feel how we feel, we tend not to appropriately express ourselves. This creates repression and sends a signal that what we are feeling is wrong.

Others may not have the same experience or the same feelings from the outcome. To someone else it may be that your feelings of elation are over reactive and it's not such a big deal. This in no way devalues your experience. For you this feels right.

There are feelings that need to be acknowledged about the journey you are making towards your outcome. How does it feel? You may feel apprehensive or you may have a feeling of excitement.

Expressing your feelings is what matters here. This helps to bring honesty to the mind. Transparency with one's self reduces the possibility of denial and self-deception.

How do I feel about my direction, goal and desired outcome (the journey and the outcome)?

Example:

I feel a little nervous about beginning to alter the way I am with people whist feeling excited about breaking through the barrier that I now see has been the most critical thing holding me back in life. I also feel it is a change I can completely control; it's entirely up to me. I feel determined to ensure that I am not allowing old habits to take root again. It is a good place to be.

~

Notes:

Question 12:

What other alternatives and possibilities exist?

Here we explore what else we might direct our mind towards. Alternatives and possibilities are what we seek. We examine the concept behind our outcome and explore other ways of getting our needs and wants met.

An example; let's say you want to be an artist. The concept might be that it allows you artistic creative expression. You could explore the possibility of researching and then learning the skill of computer graphics and accomplishing your desired outcome through a different medium.

This will require that you let your mind explore as many possibilities and alternatives as possible. Let your mind play with potential. Go lateral with your thinking; there is absolutely nothing to lose and everything to gain.

You may discover that in this section you stumble upon a great idea. Although there are tools available to further develop this skill (see the resource list in the back of this book) you can still engage with the process.

There is much to explore here. Other possibilities exist only if they are sought. As mentioned previously, your mind does not know what it does not know. You will need to show your mind what else is possible.

Avoid dismissing options until you have explored them thoroughly. It helps to engage in some lateral provocation and develop perspectives that would allow you to see and understand characteristics and behaviors previously unknown.

What other alternatives and possibilities exist? (I would suggest that you take at least ten minutes exploring this question.)

Example:

Being helpful and useful to others. Being positively playful and bringing light to those I interact with. Helping people to develop their own potential. Being strong, a rock for people I engage with. I lead interaction with people. I will nip in the bud any unwanted behavior.

~

Notes:

Question 13:

Does the goal need reviewing or redefining?

This is about taking a moment to review where you are at this point with your proposed plan for change.

Take time to consider the outcomes in terms of suitability and if it still fills your needs and wants. Altering your desired outcome is not necessarily what you will do; it's simply an option available for you to reconsider and confirm that it is indeed what you are seeking.

Perhaps you might have considered that an aspect of your needs is not being met by your current plan; it could be that an idea has come to mind that can fulfill your needs better. It could be that by altering your direction you can accomplish more of your needs and wants.

If we stay with the example of becoming an artist, it could be that by altering the outcome to computer animation, not only would there be an opportunity to express your art, it might also fulfill the need for a better income.

For you to give yourself an opportunity to validate that your desired outcome is the best one, take time to explore through reviewing your goal and tweaking where necessary. It could be that it highlights some shortfalls in the plan.

Ponder for a few minutes and consider your options. Does the planned outcome meet as many of your needs as possible? Does the plan need redefining? If it does, backtrack and refine or redefine your goal.

Does the goal need reviewing or redefining? If so how?

Example:

To develop healthy relationships, to accept others and be accepted.

~

Notes:

Question 14:

What are you *not* prepared to give up to accomplishing your goal?

Explore this question from the perspective of having to forgo or let go of something you value. Here we are talking about a cut-off point. The goal is not worth having if something of greater value is lost.

You may need to consider letting go of something temporarily or permanently in accomplishing your goal. In some instances a trade-off may be required.

This question is asked as a negative and seeks for you to consider how important your outcome is to you in relation to what already exists in your life that you may need to let go of.

This could lead to re-evaluation of your desired goal. It could be that by seeking something of value, you need to let go of something of equal or higher value.

For example if you are seeking to get into a personal relationship, you may need to let go of the social group you belong to. If the gang goes off on singles holidays it may no longer be appropriate to join them.

Or you may want to be a trainer in the private sector and leave state employment. It may be that you are not prepared to lose the security that your current employer offers. Another way may need to be found to accomplish your desire.

This question is a quick snapshot that highlights values and beliefs. It has the potential of bringing clarity to what is important in your life and consequently, what is not. Go as deep as you need to with this question.

You might also discover that the contradictions between your desires and your current comfort level cause a degree of angst. It may be that you need to work out what is important to you at this stage of life and explore the risk involved if your desired outcome is reached. What are you likely to lose?

What are you not prepared to give up by accomplishing your goal?

Example:

A certain portion of my time that is currently devoted to learning and research and personal development.

~

Notes:

Question 15:

What will not exist when you have your goal?

This question further explores changes from a perspective that seeks to look at both the negative and positive aspects in the change process.

This will allow you to spend time from the perspective of "being there" and seeing what will be missing. This further assists the mind's perception of the desired outcome.

You may be seeking to change direction in life by relocating from one city to another. What could be missing are all the local haunts, certain people, your office, friends and access to facilities. It could include your salary, security, partner, etc.

This is an opportunity to explore what will no longer be there. It may be feelings, attitudes, people, environment, etc. Remember to experience this question as if you are at your outcome.

What will not exist when you have your goal?

Example:

Loneliness, social awkwardness and social laziness. Letting people down. Fear that others can negatively influence my desires. Fear of other people's opinion of me.

~

Notes:

Question 16:

What will others experience as being different when your goal is reached?

This section covers other people's view of your accomplishment. It seeks to gain insight as to how others may experience your success.

You are in effect required to step into several people's shoes and explore what you would imagine they might observe as being different about you once you have accomplished your desired outcome.

You are seeking a sense of what others might notice as being different. For example, let's say you accomplish getting promoted at work. Stepping into the shoes of colleagues and exploring their view of your success may reveal that they notice you now care more about the business and are more communicative with them.

Your neighbors may notice that you have a company car and are dressed differently. From your partner's viewpoint, you are more self-assured and proud of your accomplishments.

In some instances you might discover that people have a negative experience as a consequence of your accomplishment. I would encourage you to seek ways to overcome these negative aspects wherever possible.

Your personal development is the priority here. In some instances it may not be possible to reconcile the effect your accomplishment has on others. Your needs are the priority here.

What will others experience as being different when your goal is reached?

Example:

Regular contact from me. A more connected friend. They will see me more often. They will perceive and sense I am more in control of my life. They will feel I am more involved in the relationship.

~

Notes:

Question 17:

Who will the experience affect when you reach your goal?

Although this question appears similar to the previous, I would encourage you to engage with it as it further validates and identifies specifically those that your goal will affect. Get into the detail.

Most of your aspirations will probably be met with praise or a degree of constructive acknowledgement. In some instances though, it may not be perceived as a constructive outcome. Some people in your life may experience your successful outcome as a loss. Consider the possibilities.

There may be a disruption dependent on the change of your outcome. It may be that you seek a different type of relationship. This may result in the person that you are currently with no longer being with you.

It could be you have decided to move into a home of your own and leave your parent's home. This may affect one or both parents. They may experience a loss.

Loss is not necessarily a bad thing. It can be useful to lose the things that cause discomfort in your life. Endings are always followed by new beginnings. This is another way of saying change.

Your loss will also create change in others. This change will impact their lives and cause them to have other experiences.

Sometimes they will be good experiences and sometimes not. Who knows?

In this section you are asked to consider those who will be affected and ponder on the effect your outcome may have on them. You are, in essence, preparing your mind to deal with such possible events.

Who will the experience affect when you reach your goal?

Example:

Everyone in my life. Some people will find that I will not be around as much whilst with others that I will be around more.

~

Notes:

Question 18:

Which attitude and mindset would best serve my needs to reach my goal?

Attitudes and mindsets are very significant in changing directions. When you consider that your existing attitudes have got you to where you are, you may understand how much they really matter.

Attitudes determine the type of journey you will experience. It is your attitude that largely sets the conditions for your experience. A negative attitude may hinder you reaching your goal.

Broadly speaking, if you have an attitude that is underpinned by some element of fear, you may inadvertently be setting yourself up for a fall. The underlying emotion is signaling danger and could cause a setback. Your experience of the journey could be marred.

Imagine setting an outcome to complete a course at college with an attitude that creates a perspective suggesting that it is going to be difficult to accomplish the outcome. You are suggesting to yourself that it will be difficult. You are unlikely to experience it as fun or easy. It is all about how you want the journey to be for you, and seeking to utilize a mindset that provides those characteristics.

Having the right mindset helps in terms of preparing yourself for the journey you are about to make. There are going to be elements that are easy, whilst others may be challenging. You might need to use a mindset that incorporates curiosity when dealing with the unknown elements that may occur.

Overconfidence and arrogance need to be weeded out when setting out to accomplish your goal. Be aware of any desperation, as it can seriously hinder progress being made. Desperate people do have a tendency to do desperate things with miserable outcomes that further fuel desperation.

Which attitude and mindset would best serve my needs to reach my goal?

Example:

Daily focus on who I need to be in touch with. Correct persistence. Treat it as a fun game to succeed at juggling all my relationships effectively, successfully and skillfully. Seek to give others pleasure and derive pleasure from others. Enjoy being more socially able, being in the driving seat.

~

Notes:

Question 19:

How can I retain any positive aspects of the past that will be affected by my reaching my goal?

There may be elements in your goal that involve some positive aspects in your current situation that you might keep. Sometimes it can be that we avoid setting a new direction on the basis that we could lose what we have and risk not having better.

It may be that you need to explore if the current desired outcome has benefits that you may want to keep. Consider if there are and if there are ways of retaining those elements.

You might be thinking of changing your job and working for a different organization. The social side of your current work may be excellent, and you might fear losing this when you change work places.

It would be prudent to spend a little time contemplating ways of maintaining the friendships you have developed. You might consider investing some of your free time meeting up with old friends. On the other hand, you could seek to fill the gap by developing new social circles as part of your planned change.

Beginnings and endings are all a part of life. No one particularly wants to end something they enjoy. This section seeks to expand awareness of some of the potential losses and design ways to incorporate them in the desired outcome to maintain them.

Some losses may be beneficial and do not require too much consideration; we are not seeking elements that are unwanted. We only seek to retain the positive aspects.

Explore a variety of ways of maintaining the benefits that are at risk or likely to be lost. As best you can, seek to design ways to incorporate them in your life once you have made the change.

How can I retain any positive aspects of the past that will be affected by my reaching my goal?

Example:

Ensure I still have some time for myself, personal contemplation, meditation and exercise, writing, etc.

~

Notes:

Question 20:

What is the most progressive step I can take to reach my goal?

Without action, plans are just plans. This section is about what actions need to be taken. The need to commit your mind to your desired outcome is paramount if you are to reach it.

To accomplish your outcome you will need to consider the stretch required to commit your mind into action. Half-hearted attempts end in negative results.

There is no "try" here. There is "do" or "not do". It is preparing and taking the most progressive step you can toward your desired outcome.

What is the greatest step? What is the most provocative movement you can make towards your outcome? What needs to happen for your mind to know how serious you are about your change of direction?

When you are standing, there are many movements you can make while still keeping your place. You can gyrate and throw your arms around and not move from the spot.

There is, though, a point of no return, when you move yourself to a place where your feet are obliged to follow. To some degree, you need to go out of balance before you find a new stability.

To activate the mind and provoke movement requires commitment. The certainty of your action validates a belief that change is inevitable. You need to be un-shifting in your need for change.

The objective is to direct your mind through your actions. Just as fishermen commit their nets into the sea, so too, you will need to commit your mind towards your outcome.

Someone seeking a new relationship has many options available and different actions they could take. They could decide that the most progressive step and most meaningful action is to get her hair done, then wait at home for something to happen. This is probably not the most productive step to take.

A man who needs to be a better manager may think that reading lots of management books is enough to make this happen. He might learn a lot of sophisticated theories about the subject. Then he waits for someone to notice how knowledgeable he is and offer him a better position.

Another person might be waiting for something to happen before they will act. They might wait for the vacancy to become available and then start the process. That could work, though consider this; they may have to wait a very long time before something becomes available.

There is little doubt that the mind will only act if it is encouraged to focus with little option for inaction. Over the years I have met many people who are stuck in the planning stage.

The tendency is to repeatedly talk about what they are going to do. Thinking about what needs to happen requires time to be set aside and thought given with large doses of common sense. Factors that need to be considered include how realistic the goal is, investment in time required, resources available, level of fear present, levels of willfulness and determination.

Airplanes, depending on their unique characteristics, need to reach an optimum speed to lift off the ground. Plans need sufficient impetus to self-activate. You are the best person to know the point you need to reach to activate the idea. You have probably done it in the past.

It is worthwhile mentioning that, having worked in this field for many years, I have noticed both in the personal therapy sector and corporate training world that all too often it is believed that the notion of being active is enough.

Activity is not necessarily productivity. "Busy doing nothing" is evidently rife for many people who believe that you must be seen to be doing something. Be clear that what you do needs to be productive. Take stock of the situations you are engaged in, and challenge your motives periodically.

What is the most progressive step that I can take to reach my goal?

Example:

Plan who I need to contact and meet each day and follow through with action.

~

Notes:

Question 21:

Mapping the known steps.

When a plan is put together there are elements that you will be aware of and others that you may not be aware of. This section deals with the steps that you are aware of.

Look at the outcome you seek and briefly remind yourself what your intention is. Stay focused on what steps you are aware of that you will need to take. These steps are the ones that you understand and are obvious to you.

For example, you might seek to qualify in some skill and need to attend a course. You may be aware that you need to register and find the funds to invest in your training.

These are facts you know, and you need to lay them out as though you were drawing a map of your journey with the elements that you are aware of.

The purpose here is to inform your mind of what steps are obvious and necessary to take, and also the steps that you may not know and that your mind will need to find solutions to. The mind does not seek solutions unless it is focused in the direction of finding solutions.

There is no need at this time to overly concern yourself with the gaps. It is important to simply be aware that there are gaps, some of which are obvious; others may not be so obvious and may only become apparent on the journey.

Mapping the known steps.
Use additional arrows where necessary.

Example

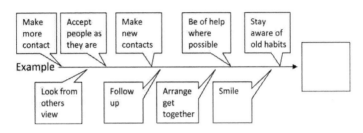

~

Notes:

Fill in your known steps.

Starting point: ──────────────────────────────➤

Question 22:

Pictorial/symbolic representation of my desired outcome.

A pictorial representation of your desired outcome helps to further embed the place you choose to reach. It is a representation and not a detailed drawing e.g. a simile, a metaphor of your intended outcome.

This could be drawn as a matchstick type of image; it could be symbols that for you represent the desired outcome. You might draw or sketch something; you could even doodle something.

There is no wrong way of doing this, there is only your way of doing this. Your way is the right way because it is what it means to you that matters. You might choose to draw an outline of a sailing vessel and a thin line to represent the shore as a way of representing a qualification in nautical navigation.

You might just draw a symbol of two hearts as representing your desire to be in a loving relationship. You could draw a big smiley face sitting behind a desk as a representation of a change of vocation. The objective is to add yet another element to your plan.

Pictorial/symbolic representation of my desired outcome.

Example:

~

Notes:

Pictorial representation.

Question 23:

How will I experience my goal?

Having got to your outcome you will have a new or different experience. This section is about re-imprinting the anticipated experience of your goal.

This may seem that it is a repetition of other sections, and in some respects it is. Yet it has a slightly different perspective in that you need to evidence to your mind that having reached your goal the experience will indeed be the one you seek and be free of unnecessary fear.

You will need to immerse yourself in the experience by passing into the future and being there as if you have accomplished your goal. A cautionary note here; you are required to complete this section once or twice thoroughly, and when you are satisfied that it is the experience you are seeking, stop.

Do avoid revisiting this as there is the possibility of stepping into the trap of hyperrealism, and it could be that your mind has tricked itself and you into thinking that it has accomplished the desired outcome.

If you are seeking a relationship, you might consider avoiding reading romantic novels. I have over the years discovered that many people are having their desires fulfilled in hyperrealism. You might find this a little challenging and it may become very difficult to stop.

Be assured that whatever you accept in hyperrealism you will not experience in reality. The choice is yours, and the talent is in the choice. Please note that to escape the trap of hyperrealism will require a high degree of determination. It can be a little like stopping a drug habit and having to deal with withdrawal.

Simply step into the required experience, explore the elements of accomplishment, accept that it is what you seek and test that this works for you.

How will I experience my goal?

Example:

Loving friends, family, business partners, clients, associates, etc. around me. Strength of perception, awareness to stop toxic relationships and people who would ridicule me.

More business and social activity in my life. More people around me. New places and experiences, a wider circle of influence. I have a greater understanding of the needs of others.

~

Notes:

Question 24:

How will I maintain and keep the benefits of my goal?

Having got to your intended outcome, there is another consideration. How do you maintain your accomplishment? In some instances there may be nothing to do other than enjoy getting to your desired outcome. In others you may need to monitor and maintain the outcome.

In most instances though, there will need to be consideration given to maintaining the outcome. If your proposed change involves getting into a relationship with a life partner, you may need to consider what will be required to maintain it.

You may need to consider things like the time you will need to devote to the activities you engage in, the interest you will develop together and the emotional closeness; otherwise the relationship may soon lose its spark if you leave it unattended.

Designing and creating a garden is a pleasure for some people. It will soon be lost unless it is maintained. It is no different with some of the outcomes that you may seek.

You could be seeking an outcome to become a supervisor in a sales call centre. Once you are there what will need to happen for you to maintain that position?

It could be that there is little to do to maintain that position; it could be that you will need to invest in your ongoing professional development; or it could be that you will need to develop new skill sets such as better interpersonal relationships.

How will I maintain and keep the benefits of my goal?

Example:

I will need to be organized, keeping on top of this goal and my new habits continually. I will need to be aware of my personal energy levels and health and create a balance where I still look after myself and my relaxation. I will need to root out any old negative habits by regularly screening for them in my behavior.

~

Notes:

Question 25:

Will a fallback position better motivate me?

Sometimes we have difficulty in completely committing to making change. It seems when it involves an element of risk, the fear experienced can stop us in our tracks. Inaction becomes the rule. It is understandable in this day and age when the fear peddled by so many people is constant.

There is a barrage of messages bombarding our everyday life from the media, government, businesses, etc. It's tough not to dismiss it. We are becoming incapable of making any changes unless we are told that they are the right thing to do.

If we get it wrong, ridicule finishes us off. The fear of making a significant change in our personal or professional life can overwhelm us and keep us stuck. This applies more so in the European world and not so much in the United States of America where praise is given for having a go.

"The American lives even more for his goals, for the future, than the European. Life for him is always becoming, never being."

Albert Einstein

European culture has this unfortunate characteristic, and those who realize it is not personal deal with it differently. Those who buy into the notion that you have to succeed at everything you do the first time live mostly in fear. The fear of failure and the ridicule that may follow paralyses most people.

The situation is further complicated for those who are unclear about designing a plan to change an element of their life. Armed only with their history, some people have good reason to stay put and avoid the possibility of repeating past failures. They are not able to see that we need to design a way forward.

For some, creating a change in their life is impeded by the notion that the only way is up and, unless their position takes them to a more secure place, they are happy enough to stay put. Sometimes we need to make a lateral move to change direction.

There are several options to be considered here prior to moving to the next section.

You may have reservations and need a buffer zone; you might feel more prone to create a change if you could have a fallback position in place. You could start a process for change in parallel to what you are engaged in and know that it will not affect your current position.

This may not always be possible and is largely determined by the outcome you seek. This may enhance your feelings of calm by enabling you to reduce the chances of failing whilst still heading toward your goal.

Consider a particular aspect of your history related to getting your needs and wants met. Are there areas in the past where you have delayed action only to see the opportunity be taken by someone else, or lost an opportunity and only then realized that it was something you could have done?

Perhaps if you had a fallback position you might have had a go at getting there. You may prefer to go all the way and not give your mind an opportunity to go for the easy option. "All or nothing" personality traits tend to want it as they want it or not at all. Half-hearted attempts are not on their agenda.

In some instances, it may be that the fallback position is the outcome and the declared outcome is just a long shot. You would need to consider this carefully when designing your future outcomes. Avoid confusing your mind with unclear or mixed messages. Keep it clear and concise so the goal becomes easier to identify.

The objective in this section is to consider having a fallback position set up that would make your commitment easer to engage with. It is not always possible to have a fallback position, so this is suggested in situations if there is a need and where it is possible to have a fallback position.

You might, for example, apply for work in a different organization and keep your options open with your existing employer. Many do this and are able to maintain a position until they have accomplished their goal.

This is acceptable as it enables you to create a safety net. You get to keep your job whilst seeking a better position with another company. This is acceptable, though keep in mind that certain shifts require a termination of one process for the commencement of another.

Common sense rules need to apply here. There is little point in doing something that creates a situation that could be damaging to an individual. The care of health and the effect on ones emotional and psychological state is important.

You might want to go out on a date with someone you like and so arrange for someone else to make the enquiry as to that person's availability and interest before taking the step yourself.

In that case it could be that the fear of rejection overwhelms you and paralyses any possible action. It is less risky having someone else do the asking for you and can soften the blow of rejection should it occur.

The fear of getting it wrong and failing can be so frightening that for many people the outcome is not worth the cost. You could argue that if there is no risk there may be a reduction in value.

For some people having a fallback position is not an option. For those people, second best or compromise does not work and it is not an option. Perhaps this is due to the lack of the necessary tension to stimulate their drivers into action.

You might find that you cannot deal with second best. You would rather stay where you are than not have it all. Perhaps an "all or nothing personality trait" is the way that works for you.

It seems that whatever happens, with or without having a fallback position, the motivation to change requires a degree of tension that only you know will get you to create change.

Will a fallback position better motivate me? If "yes", define it.

Example:

No.

~

Notes:

Question 26:

What are my concerns with my choice of goal?

This section explores a little deeper the nature of any concerns that you may still have. There is a degree of risk with any directed change. It is useful to explore the concerns raised by the risk. It may be that for some outcomes there is virtually no risk. If there is a win-win situation just keep going. Where there is a degree of risk, ponder on the question.

Just take some time to consider the desired outcome, review your journey and consider if your concerns for your choice have increased, decreased or stayed the same.

It may be that for you everything is as it was. The desired outcome is as you want it and your concern is at a level you can manage.

You might notice that the level of concern is increased. You might sense the outcome to be a little more challenging and this may create a concern.

In this case, review your outcome and focus on what you perceive as the specific areas of concern. Consider these concerns and seek to discover ways of minimizing them.

Think about where your attention needs to be focused and apply your mind to untangling the concerns, address them individually and move on.

Ensure that you are dealing with concerns that can be addressed at this junction and not concerns that cannot be dealt with until you are there to deal with them.

Some things cannot be dealt with until they are in front of you. Only then will you know how to deal with them. So, as you think of any concerns, take a moment to differentiate between the concerns that you can overcome or reduce and the ones that may arise in the future.

What are my concerns with my choice of goal?

Example:

That some part of my old beliefs will scupper my progress.

~

Notes:

Question 27:

Is the goal worth the cost in terms of time, finance and energy?

There is little, if anything, that we do that does not benefit us directly or indirectly on some level. Most actions are designed to produce a reward; at least that is the intention.

We tend the garden because it gives us pleasure at some level or reduces a fear at another. In either case the action is taken to produce a desired outcome.

Sometimes the reward comes at a cost that is not fully considered. It may be that we are putting in far more than the outcome is worth. Only we can decide the value.

In everyday life we may notice this from people who charge ahead with an idea, only to find that by the time they get to it the sense of victory they might have expected is in fact a feeling of failure.

It's important to pay attention to the cost of getting to an outcome. The question that needs pondering is whether the cost is worth the outcome. To put it even more simply, is this worth doing?

There are several aspects to consider here that may affect your drive. You could possibly experience your outcome not as intended. It would be useful to focus on these aspects if they include cost in terms of time, finance, energy and other resources.

As with any passage, change comes with time. Time needs to be seen as the greatest investment. Time, once spent, cannot be re-acquired as, say, money could. Once spent, time stays spent. It needs to be treated with great respect and consideration given to its true value.

Time has the ability to create most other resources but cannot create itself. Once you have experienced this moment, you cannot go back to it. You can only remember it, which itself uses time.

It is important to consider time as a value when reaching for your desired action. Indecision is great at stealing time. Be aware and learn skills that help to create a more decisive you.

Having said this, the time it takes to consider an action is also critical when evaluating an outcome. There is a degree of time needed in making a decision and implementing the decision.

Some things can be time consuming and others not. Just be mindful that you are aware of the cost in time and perhaps consider if it is worth the cost to you.

Another consideration is financial cost. It may be that your desired outcome requires a financial investment. If you are seeking to gain a better qualification in your field, you will need to consider that there may be a cost involved.

It may be that there is a fee for this qualification. It may be that you need to take time out and consequently live with a lower income for a while. It may be that you are planning to move to another location and this may add to your cost of travel.

There are many considerations here, though this does not apply to all desired outcomes, as some may not involve a financial cost. If you wanted to study and go to the library, this doesn't involve a payment.

It is worthwhile just pondering on the financial side of your outcome and getting as many of the facts as possible. Be aware and reduce the possibility of any unpleasant surprises.

The financial cost requires thinking through so be as informed as you can be. This section is about taking the opportunity to explore the financial consequences of this desired outcome.

Another consideration is your energy levels. You may have an abundance of energy and be raring to go; It may be that you are not so physically active; it may also be that you are lacking in emotional energy.

We can increase our energy levels by eating quality foods and exercising our mind and muscles. We can increase our mental energy by keeping our minds flexible through developing better thinking skills and learning to play lateral exercises and by introducing more humor into life.

This section requires you to consider your energy levels. It is critical that you have sufficient energy to start and maintain your desired outcome. If not you will need to plan a goal to bring your strengths up to a standard that will assist in getting you to your goal.

We need also to consider that in most instances the journey provides us with rewards en route that tops up our psychological and emotional energy. The rewards are like little emotional oasis' that lift our spirits and helps us stay motivated toward the outcome.

When we are down we are more prone to be active in our pursuit of change. Energy levels are depleted by the degree of intensity applied to a task. The more intense, the more energy is used. It's a little like driving a car with your foot down on the accelerator. The more fuel used, the more pressure the engine experiences. There is an optimum that needs to be found.

Where the outcome is filled with the right reward, we do feel empowered and have the drive for completion. You may have had the experience of seeking a relationship in your early years and walking, talking and staying up until late or going out of your way to bump into someone. The right goal with the promise of a good outcome gives us the strength to follow it.

When energy is lacking, our disposition changes as the mind seeks to conserve what it has and rebuilds the resources. Pacing ourselves is important if we are to accomplish our objective.

Energy is limited and can vary with our health, age and attitude. Our attitude is a little like the quality of fuel we use in a car. The better the quality the further we go. Attitude and energy are to some degree related as far as the mind is concerned.

Once we engage in the process the mind, with directions and conviction, will search to acquire more en route if we seek it. Some people are energized when things are going well; others can be deflated easily when things are not. You just need to watch a sports event to see the effect on the losing team and the winning team.

Other considerations include your network of friends, colleagues and associations that may assist you in acquiring your desired outcome.

Is the goal worth the cost in terms of time, finance and energy?

Example:

Ensure I balance my energy by still taking care and looking after myself. Yes, the goal is definitely worth the cost.

~

Notes:

Question 28:

What will my next goal be about?

The focus goes beyond the target. Here we seek to discover what the next outcome will be in the broadest sense. The target is accepted as accomplished and we seek to show the mind what will happen thereafter.

This may play a small part in your drive to accomplish your outcome. Your mind may be sufficiently activated with the task at hand.

Others may need to see beyond the outcome and give an indication as to what the next goal will be. In some ways this shows that there is more to come. This, I believe, gives the mind the belief that if you are already thinking past this outcome and you are going to the next then the current goal is a certainty.

If you are the type of person who needs to be constantly active, your mind needs to see that it will continue to be active once you have accomplished your outcome. The pain of boredom may be so strong that the idea of an outcome being set which may result in inactivity could be scuttled.

Look ahead and sense what you will be striving for next. Get the big picture in your mind. Show yourself that you are thinking about the next part of your accomplishment. It may be possible that the mind joins up the dots easier when there is more.

Set a future goal in place for the purpose of giving your mind the certainty of continuation.

What will my next outcome be? (In a nutshell and without the need to justify)

Example:

To develop a successful business.

~

Notes:

Question 29:

Have my feelings changed with my choice of goal?

Now it is time to explore your emotional and psychological state about your goal. This section is addressing your senses and only your senses. It is just interested in how you feel now about your desired outcome.

Have your feelings changed? Is there more enthusiasm to reach your outcome? Do you need to adjust your outcome because the reward is insufficient? Does your outcome need more clarity? Do you need more information? These are the questions that need to be pondered.

The difference here is that you are seeking only your senses' response to these questions. What do you feel about it? Only your feelings matter here.

Getting a sense of having your outcome can also include your intuition. Intuition is perhaps the output of your mind's amalgamated learning that cannot be easily quantified.

Have my feelings changed with my choice of goal?

Example:

There is more enthusiasm to reach my outcome. I feel that it is very much obtainable; I need to keep my awareness up and continue taking the right actions.

~

Notes:

Question 30:

Simply explore your feelings and check to notice if they have changed.

This section seeks to check the driver behind your desired outcome. Notice if your feelings have altered or have changed since you first checked them in question 11.

As mentioned previously, we are all driven by either fear of something happening that would cause us pain, or by pleasure (more precisely the pursuit of joy).

Transparency is essential here. There is nothing worse than self-deception. Be honest with yourself as to the motivation behind your action.

It may be that when you started this process the journey was born of fear and your concern was that if you did not take some action you would experience a degree of pain.

It might also be that as you journey through the change process you are beginning to perceive that your mind has the capability to create a very different future from the one you are experiencing, and that there is no reason whatsoever for you not to have it.

To move from fear to excitement, as a driving force behind your action, would be extremely beneficial both on a psychological level and on a physical level.

When driven by fear, we can experience stress and, in some instances, distress. On the other hand, when driven by pleasure, we can experience *eu-stress*, a healthy, life-giving, exciting energy.

Simply explore your feelings and check to notice if they have changed. Are they the same, have they deteriorated or are they more optimistic? Just describe them as best you can.

Example:

Positive, focused, excited and in the zone

~

Notes:

Validation:

This section is to conclude the process. Having set a new direction for change, all that remains is a final check. This is to provide you with external feedback and helps commit your mind to the journey.

The goal you have chosen to direct your mind towards needs another perspective to ensure that it is in keeping with your best interests. You have invested time in planning, and it is helpful for your mind to have clear direction for the outcome you seek. Now you have looked beyond to what the next step will likely be.

"Give me six hours to chop a tree and I will spend the first four sharpening the axe".

Abraham Lincoln

Taking time to design the way forward will make the journey more likely to conclude with you reaching a successful outcome.

This section asks you to choose a person in your life who you sense is balanced, pragmatic and able to express his or her thoughts and feelings about your choice of outcome.

Ask this person to check your timings and anticipated rewards. It needs to be someone who has integrity and who you do not have any serious reason to distrust.

The individual does not need to be a close friend or relative, I might advise against choosing someone who is too close, unless it is someone who you can evidence cares for you and your development.

Here you will be seeking someone to review your proposed journey and to ensure that there are no obvious gaps in your planning. He or she will need to be caring enough to ask the questions that another may prefer not to ask. Choose someone who has evidenced a degree of sound decision making and is reasoned in their thinking.

On a different level, there is an additional benefit to employ the services of another. It may be that your written word witnessed by another person creates an obligation to complete the task.

If you have the type of personality that is more connected to accomplishing something after you have given your word to that effect, the embarrassment of having to forsake your desired outcome may just be a little too much.

The individual you choose to help you with this section needs to understand what you are planning and be able to see the seriousness of your desired outcome. Your goal is important to you. It could well be a life-changing direction that you have selected, and it needs to be treated with respect.

The change for you is personal and meaningful. It is important to you and you cannot have someone belittling your plan.

Find a person who has a degree of kindness and strength, who can see your potential and encourages your idea, someone who can connect with you and is level-headed. It can be a parent or sibling, a teacher, a school friend, a colleague, a mentor, a coach, etc.

Ridicule is possible and needs to be minimized or eradicated from having access to your mind. I would suggest that you share your desired outcome with others on a need-to-know basis. Reveal your goals only when you have achieved them.

There is another interesting aspect to keeping your goal out of the public domain. You may have met people who seem to talk a great deal about what they are going to do. They are able to keep everyone entertained by their future exploits. For them that's enough. The talk is not the walk.

What matters most is that you respect the person you choose. It should be someone whose values, judgment and critique you hold in esteem. Accepting that, you can accept their opinion, as it is designed to help you.

Ensure that the person you select has nothing to lose from your gain. It will hinder or mar your process if this person experiences an involuntary bias against your plan.

Just as a point of interest, respect and fear can sometimes be confused. You may fear someone yet have no respect for them. You can respect someone whilst experiencing a degree of fear.

You will need to invite the person you choose to review your desired outcome. He or she will first need to read it through in its entirety then restart and go through section by section and ponder on your answers without asking for detail. He or she should give observational feedback to you.

This person may make suggestions to you; he or she may ask for clarification or suggest whether the time you have given to the project is unrealistic and needs increasing or decreasing.

The objective is to give you a reality check, to help you see that it is not just pie in the sky or a dream you cannot make into reality.

Remember that it is only someone else's opinion. It is meant to help you to confirm that your outcome is achievable. Where this person cannot understand something, help him or her and clarify the point.

If the person you chose still does not understand, imagine it as he or she does and then help to clarify understanding. Glean as much as you can from the opportunity.

In the event that there is no one who can do this with you, as a last resort you may need to take on this role yourself. In that case, you will need to look at the process as though you were advising a friend. In this event, avoid doing the process on the same day as you complete it.

Please read through the next section prior to handing your work for validation.

Validation:

I have read through the process and conclude that it is achievable.

Name:: ....

Date   ____:_____:_____

Congratulations on a great accomplishment. Having completed the change process, you can now take some time and allow your mind to rest and realign and begin to change direction.

The Way Forward

The process that you have been involved in is now ready to be put into action. You will need to take the most progressive step you can. Your time and timing is important.

Sometimes it's easier to work backwards from your desired outcome. If, for example, you need to have your goal completed six months from today, where will you need to be in five months, in four months, in three months, in two months, by the end of this month? See if you can get a general sense of how things could unfold.

There is a time and a place in life for most things. Everything has its time and there is a time for everything.

Occasionally, there are times when we want something to happen and are left feeling disappointed when it does not. Looking back, however, we are often relieved that something we thought we wanted never materialized.

Occasionally there is a misfire; it's just not the right time or the best outcome. Things in life can be a little bit like that. Life, after all, to a degree is predictably unpredictable.

Just as good things happen and land in our laps, those things may occasionally fall in the wrong place. At times, this can work in our favor; at others, not.

Be curious about change and how to design and implement change. The more you can direct that change, the greater control you have of your journey through life. Total control is unrealistic.

Avoid being too attached to the outcome if you begin to notice any degree of desperation. The more relaxed about it you can be, the less energy you waste.

Change, in any event, will occur with or without your direction. I cannot guarantee you of much else, but I can assure of this.

When change can be seen as inevitable, it makes sense to engage with it. Direct it to best serve you and humanity. Communicating your needs and wants to yourself and striving for better in your life is the first step, and all that is required now is to simply design a way of getting there.

It isn't necessary for something to be wrong for you to seek better by designing a better way forward. There is no conflict whatsoever if you decide to enjoy what exists in your life whilst planning the next step. In fact, you are designing future events for you to enjoy.

"Be who you are and say what you feel because those who mind don't matter and those who matter don't mind."

Dr. Seuss

Keep in mind that you cannot not communicate both to others and to yourself. It is impossible not to communicate. If you do not call someone, you are communicating that you are not calling. When you are not talking to someone, you are communicating silence.

If both your inner and outer worlds are receiving a communication from you, it would be wise to decide what that communication is going to be.

Take time to think of the things that would benefit you if they were possible. Explore what could happen if you did something different.

Change is what creates life, so be part of the change.

The benefits of this process are numerous. It would be easy to miss out on some of the more subtle rewards that life has to offer.

Your journey will help build your skills and build more character. Your journey will help you recognize areas that you can develop. These might include better communication skills, advanced thinking skills and better decision making, etc.

It is highly likely that you will develop a thirst for knowledge and a better understanding of how your mind works. There are several books and resources that I have included at the back of this book for your consideration.

I would encourage you to be constantly on the lookout for practical ideas and thinking tools that will help you navigate better through life. Look out for people who exhibit large doses of common sense in what they are doing. Study them, learn from them, understand them and then use what you have learnt at the first possible opportunity.

The better you are able to understand what to pay attention to and what to ignore, the better your navigational abilities will become. Stay aware and remain focused on the opportunities that will present themselves to you and that you are not distracted too far from your needs and wants.

A point to consider is that some things in life are outside of our field of influence. There are situations that are outside of our control. It may be that we are enrolled in or committed to a situation that has fixed rules. Sometimes we simply need to ride the storm until a situation arises where we can influence a change in direction.

There are endless opportunities available in life, and where there are not, there may be an opportunity to create some. We always have the option of moving to a place that allows for more opportunities. It is all about being aware that you always have choice.

Much of life is unknown. At best you can come to grips with the bit of life that you exist in, your reality, that place you can best describe to yourself and others. The potentials are endless.

If you like certain aspects of it then you may want more; if you do not you can choose to create change. It does not matter in what area of your life you want to change. Design something, create something or change something that will bring more pleasure in your life.

Just remember to be practical in your thinking, pragmatic in your actions and focused in your quest for more. There is plenty of room for a little risk.

"Only those who will risk going too far can possibly find out how far one can go."

T.S. Eliot

Something for you to consider as you design your change journey is you may notice that you begin to recognize other people's situations far better than you may have done in the past. I would advise extreme caution if you should choose to point out their pattern of behavior to them.

Remember that they probably have not read this book, and the possibility is that they will defend their position or attack your view. There is also the risk of alienating them from you.

"You gave him an opportunity of showing greatness of character and he did not seize it. He will never forgive you for that."

Friedrich Wilhelm Nietzsche

The best way to inspire movement in others is through your own accomplishment. Those who will be inspired are those who you could have best helped. You could treat them to a copy of this book.

Having completed your plan, you simply need to put your book away and start the journey. Only refer to your plan on a need-to-review basis. You can, however, reread the first section of the book to refresh your mind periodically.

There is further information on my Website to assist you in selecting approved training. Feel free to leave comments of your successes on my blog found at:
www.change-directions.com.
I would love to hear of your accomplishments.
Stop reading about changing directions and start doing.

Remember…enjoy the journey.

Recommended Books

Teach Yourself to Think
ISBN: 978 0 14 023077 2
Edward de Bono

Edward De Bono's Thinking Course
ISBN: 978 0 56 3522041
Edward de Bono

Lateral Thinking
ISBN: 978 0 14 0137798
Edward de Bono

The Six Thinking Hats
ISBN: 978 0 14 0296662
Edward de Bono

Think - Before It's Too Late
ISBN: 978 0 09 1924096
Edward de Bono

The Six Value Medals
ISBN: 978 0 09 1894597
Edward de Bono

Textbook of Wisdom
ISBN: 978 0 67 0870110
Edward de Bono

My Little Book of Verbal Antidotes
ISBN: 978 0 95 3666706
Georges Philips and Tony Jennings

My Little Book of Neuro Linguistic Programming
ISBN: 978 0 95 3000775
Tony Jennings and Georges Philips

It's Not How Good You Are, It's How Good You Want to Be
ISBN: 978 0 71 4843377
Paul Arden

How to Have a Beautiful Mind
ISBN: 978 0 09 1894603
Edward de Bono

Stop Thinking, Start Living
ISBN: 978 0 72 253547
Richard Carlson

As a Man Thinketh
ISBN: 978 0 89471 714
James Allen

Screw Work Lets Play
ISBN: 978 0 273 73093 4
John Williams

Good to Great
ISBN-13: 978-0712676090
Jim Collins

For more detailed knowledge readers may find the following useful.

Gold Psychotherapeutic Counselling
ISBN: 978 1 89 9836338
A Structured Psychotherapeutic Approach to the Mapping
and Re-Aligning of Belief Systems.
Georges Philips and Lyn Buncher

The Mechanism of Mind
ISBN: 978 0 14 0214451
Edward de Bono
(Available used only.)

Introducing NLP (Neuro-Linguistic Programming)
ISBN: 978 1 85 5383449
Joseph O'Connor and John Seymour

The Blank Slate
ISBN: 978 0 14 0276053
Steven Pinker

The Stuff of Thought
ISBN: 978 0 14 1015477
Steven Pinker

The Sourcebook of Magic
ISBN: 978 1 89 983622
L. Michael Hall and Barbara P. Belnap

Other books with Georges Philips:

Gold Counselling 2nd edition

Rapid Cognitive Therapy Vol. 1

Analytical Hypnotherapy Vol. 1

Analytical Hypnotherapy Vol. 2

My Little Book of Verbal Antidotes (Kindle/E-Pub)

My Little Book of Neuro Linguistic Programming (Kindle/E-Pub)

My Little Book of Meditation (Kindle/E-Pub)

The ONE diet

Books in progress

Self Management

Hand of Leadership

Additional training and facilitating is available from:

www.change-directions.com

This site includes articles, blogs and details of forthcoming workshops and seminars. You can also follow on:
www. http://twitter.com/#!/ChgDirs
www.facebook.com/changedirections
E-mail: info@change-directions.com

www.georgesphilips.com

My site offers a selection of training and support from teaching the de Bono thinking tools to belief restructuring, coaching, mentoring and bespoke facilitation. Contact my office directly with your enquires info@georgesphilips.com

TheONEdiet.com

This Website is filled with information and advice for anyone seeking help and clarity on nutrition and fitness issues. As well as publishing an informative blog, it offers helpful downloads and previews products and is a source of quality links to professional Websites and more.

www.edwarddebono.com

This Website offers a range of online training in the de Bono thinking methodology and is a great source of quotes and interesting articles for those seeking to improve their knowledge base.

www.cortthinking.com

The site offers lessons in thinking for those interested in developing better thinking skills. CoRT is the complete thinking course developed in Cambridge University by Dr. Edward de Bono.

Priority Value Matrix

In the event that you have a number of options, it may help to make a quick evaluation and assess the most beneficial way forward for you.

Simply write in the options and score along side. See example.

The matrix provides a simple solution to finding the most efficient way forward. It is by no means designed to deal with some of the more serious areas of change you may want to make in your life. The matrix is used to explore relatively simple changes.

Example:

Options	Ease of Doing	Cost of Doing	Time Required	Pleasure or Relief in Doing	Total	Priority Ranking
1 Learn to play the guitar.	1	9	3	9	22	2
2 Learn Spanish	3	9	3	9	24	1
3 Start an internet business	3	3	1	3	10	3

Options	Ease of Doing	Cost of Doing	Time Required	Pleasure or Relief in Doing	Total	Priority Ranking
1						
2						
3						
4						
5						
6						

Ease of doing:	Cost of doing:	Time required:	Pleasure or relief in doing:
9 = Almost nothing	9 = Almost nothing	9 = Little or no time	9 = A great deal
3 = Some	3 = Some	3 = Moderate cost	3 = Some
1 = A great deal	1 = A great deal	1 = High cost	1 = Almost nothing

Some examples of areas for change that you may want to explore:

Be in a relationship

Accept people

Laugh more

Listen better

Be more communicative

Better communication with people

Create more income

Be more engaging

Be more certain

Develop a new skill

Learn a new language

Improve my reading skill

Improve a marriage/partnership

Write better

Get on better with colleagues

Be a great leader

Inspire people

Pass my driving tests

Develop new skills

Be more open

Travel to more places

Reach a certain weight

Be a good cook

Stay calm

Be a good manager

Be transparent

Appreciate more

Write a book

Enjoy a sport

Live a healthy life

Stay focused

Be married

Be a great presenter

Research efficiently

Develop good relationships with my child/children

Learn how to think well

Pass exams